Art Activities
from
Folk & Fairy Tales

Written and illustrated by Judy Hierstein

Teaching & Learning Company

1204 Buchanan St., P.O. Box 10
Carthage, IL 62321

This book belongs to

_____

Cover photo by Images and More Photography

Copyright © 1996, Teaching & Learning Company

ISBN No. 1-57310-045-5

Printing No. 987654321

Teaching & Learning Company
1204 Buchanan St., P.O. Box 10
Carthage, IL 62321

The purchase of this book entitles teachers to make copies for use in their individual classrooms, only. This book, or any part of it, may not be reproduced in any form for any other purposes without prior written permission from the Teaching & Learning Company. It is strictly prohibited to reproduce any part of this book for an entire school or school district, or for commercial resale.

All rights reserved. Printed in the United States of America.

Table of Contents

Materials, Sources, Recipes 1

To Begin 3

Puss in Boots Illustrated by Fred Marcellino, written by Charles Perrault and translated by Malcolm Arthur 4

Little Red Riding Hood Illustrated and retold by Trina Schart Hyman 7

Goldilocks and the Three Bears Illustrated and retold by Jan Brett 11

The Sleeping Beauty Illustrated and retold by Mercer Mayer 14

The Three Billy Goats Gruff Illustrated and retold by Paul Galdone 18

Rumpelstiltskin Illustrated and retold by Paul O. Zelinsky 22

Hansel and Gretel Illustrated and retold by James Marshall 26

Jack and the Beanstalk Illustrated and retold by Steven Kellogg 30

The Three Little Pigs and the Big Bad Wolf Illustrated and retold by Glen Rounds 33

The Gingerbread Man Illustrated by Megan Lloyd and retold by Eric A. Kimmel 37

Strega Nona Illustrated and retold by Tomie de Paola 41

Beauty and the Beast Illustrated and retold by Warwick Hutton 44

Henny Penny Illustrated and retold by Paul Galdone 48

Snow White Illustrated by Angela Barrett and retold by Josephine Poole 52

The Rainbabies Illustrated by Jim LaMarche and written by Laura Krauss Melmed 55

Swamp Angel Illustrated by Paul O. Zelinsky and written by Anne Isaacs 59

Thumbelina Illustrated by Susan Jeffers, written by Hans Christian Andersen and retold by Amy Ehrlich 63

The Pied Piper of Hamelin Illustrated by Annegert Fuchshuber, written by Robert Browning and retold by Barbara Bartos-Höppner 67

The Bremen Town Musicians Illustrated and retold by Josef Paleček, written by the Brothers Grimm and translated by Anthea Bell 71

The Ugly Duckling Illustrated and retold by Lorinda Bryan Cauley and written by Hans Christian Andersen 75

Cinderella Illustrated and translated by Marcia Brown and written by Charles Perrault 79

The Little Lame Prince Illustrated and retold by Rosemary Wells, based on a story by Dinah Maria Mulock Craik 83

Rapunzel Illustrated by Trina Schart Hyman, retold by Barbara Rogasky and written by the Brothers Grimm 86

The Frog Prince Continued Illustrated by Steve Johnson and written by Jon Scieszka 89

The Dragon 92

Dear Teacher,

With the elementary art teacher becoming an endangered species, the classroom teacher is frequently expected to provide her class with the only art the class may have. For those with very little background and experience in the subject, this can be an uncomfortable responsibility. This book can help.

While teaching elementary art classes, I have found that one of the most effective ways of presenting an art lesson is by using picture books. There is no easier way to hold a class' attention than to read them a story, and with the profusion of books available in this "Golden Age of Children's Literature," it is not difficult to find just the right one to fit your needs—it is most likely already in your classroom or school library—and leave your students eager to begin work.

Children's books today are illustrated with superb art, often reflecting current trends in the art world or emulating the artistic style of the period when the story takes place, or the ethnic style of the culture where it takes place. Students are exposed to fine art, perhaps the first time, through these books. The illustrations are usually impeccably researched for authenticity, filled with visual side stories, foreshadowing and subtle detail (often humorous) discovered after repeated viewings.

Many picture books of today are well-loved folk and fairy tales retold and illustrated to appeal to a new generation of children. The term *folktale* generally refers to a story which has been told and retold by common folk through the years, changing with each telling to suit the audience. Eventually, someone would write it down and publish it. Sometimes an author, such as Hans Christian Andersen, created an original story in the form of a folktale, which with time, took its place among old favorites. Though the precise definition may be sketchy, the value of these tales is clear. They can help us to understand the beliefs of a culture during a period of time, as well as human instincts that are basic to all cultures and times. The stories are good, simple and fast moving. They contain themes and illusions which will reappear later in adult literature. They teach us to use our imaginations to dream about the possibilities that we may one day turn into reality.

In this book, I have selected some of my favorite versions of folk and fairy tales from our European heritage and created solid art extension activities which have proven successful in my artroom and will be successful in your classroom. Each activity begins with a short summary of the tale and comments about the story and illustrations. Then an art activity is explained, complete with a list of the materials required, step-by-step illustrated directions, the art concepts and techniques involved, artists whose work is related to that of the illustrator, and suggestions for arranging the finished projects into effective displays. I've designed these activities so that they utilize classroom supplies normally on hand. In most cases substitutions may be made that will not damage the integrity of the lesson. Also included are tips on acquiring materials free or inexpensively, and recipes for homemade art materials.

With this whole language approach, students grow to love the traditional literature of their own and other cultures as they become acquainted with important concepts and techniques of various art forms. I hope you find the ideas in this book as useful and fun as I have.

Sincerely,

Judy

Judy Hierstein

Materials, Sources, Recipes

Our community has a program called WasteSHARE, whose mission is to recycle materials that businesses and industries would throw away, making these materials available to teachers free of charge. The school system has provided space in their maintenance building and teachers go there during specified hours and help themselves, free of charge. The director receives a salary for which she contacts businesses, collects and stores materials, and keeps track of what is utilized. Originally the program was funded by a grant, but now each school system that participates in the program is asked to pay the small fee of $1.00 per student in their district to cover the salary of the director so the program is self-sufficient. Everyone agrees this is a great program—especially teachers who can enrich their curriculum without impoverishing themselves.

At the beginning of the school year, usually during Open House, I send a letter to the parents asking them to save any supplies we may use. My list of suggested supplies includes: anything shiny (wrappers from chocolate bars, mylar chips bags, aluminum foil); used gift wrap; ribbons; cardboard toilet paper and paper towel rolls; Styrofoam™ trays (Be sure they are washed to avoid contamination from previous contents. These make excellent containers for storing scissors, crayons and other art supplies. They also can be used for printmaking. Even the youngest student can safely press lines into the soft surface or cut to make dragon or butterfly wings.); old greeting cards—especially holiday cards because they often have shiny surfaces; used fabric softener sheets from the dryer; plastic containers; egg cartons. (These make perfect tempera paint containers. Each work table gets a small amount of color in the individual egg indentations in the carton. Spare indentations and extra cartons can be used for creative color mixing, and at the end of the project the nearly empty cartons can simply be tossed into the trash for easy cleanup. Sometimes the used egg cartons look like superb examples of abstract sculpture.)

- Most home decorating shops are happy to give away wallpaper sample books once they are outdated. Stop by and leave your name and phone number so the owner can call you when books are available. Wallpaper samples are easier for young students to cut than fabric, yet they provide the same visual interest as printed cloth does, and often it is shiny, sheeny or opalescent.

- Inquire at the hospital for old sheets that have become too worn to use. These will have been laundered and sterilized so they are perfectly safe. They can be cut into small individual banners, tie-dyed, printed or used whole for bodies of Chinese dragons or quilts.

- Our local mall conducts promotions throughout the year and uses many posters printed on expensive, heavy poster board or foamcore. Once the promotion is over, the posters are useless to the mall so they are happy to donate them to schools. They cut easily on the paper cutter and take paint well to make everything from medieval shields to African masks and pendants, to bases for three-dimensional scenes.

- There are several large printing companies in our area who are willing to give us paper scraps, which are sometimes quite large and usually of higher quality than school-grade paper. They can be cut on a paper cutter to fit your specifications.

- Before I throw anything away, I consider whether I may be able to use it on an art project.

Recipes

Cooked Dough

    1 c. (240 ml) flour
    1/2 c. (120 ml) salt
    1 c. (240 ml) water
    2 tsp. (10 ml) cream of tartar
    1 T. (15 ml) vegetable oil
    food coloring (optional)

Combine ingredients and cook over medium heat, stirring constantly, especially when mixture begins to thicken. Turn out onto waxed paper and cover with plastic until dough is cool enough to handle. Keep the dough inside a plastic bag to prevent drying. Food coloring may be added with the other ingredients (less messy) or kneaded in at anytime after the clay is prepared to achieve a greater variety of colors. Pastel colors work best, and the three shades: yellow, rose or magenta, and turquoise or cyan, can be mixed to make all the colors in the color wheel.

Salt Clay

    1 c. (240 ml) salt
    1 c. (240 ml) flour
    1 T. (15 ml) alum
    food coloring (optional)

Mix with enough water to form clay or putty consistency. Store in plastic bags to prevent drying. Food coloring may be added, but it is better to paint the sculpture after it has dried.

Chunky Egg Carton Clay

Tear paper egg cartons into 1" (2.5 cm) square pieces and soak them overnight in a large plastic container. Drain and squeeze out all excess moisture; then pour in white glue and mix with hands until mixture is the consistency of clay. This clay works well for lunar and terrestrial landscapes and may be painted once dry.

Smooth Egg Carton or Newspaper Clay

If a smoother consistency of clay is required for projects such as dragons or finger puppets, place egg carton pieces or wet strips of newspaper in an old blender until it is half full. Add enough water to cover. Pulverize, then drain through a colander, squeeze to remove all excess moisture and mix with white glue until the consistency of clay is achieved. (On occasions when I have needed a little extra clay quickly, I have unrolled toilet paper, dampened it and added the white glue.) With any of these materials, the resulting clay sticks well to cardboard rolls or boxes which may be incorporated into the sculpture, and takes tempera paint beautifully once dry. There is a commercial product on the market called Celluclay™ to which you merely add water. It is a lot less work but more expensive.

Marbleized Paper

Thin small amounts (1 tsp. [5 ml]) of oil paint with 1 T. (15 ml) turpentine so that it reaches the consistency of water. Use an old brush and a baby food jar for each color. Fill a shallow foil roasting pan half full of water. Pour a few drops of the thinned paint onto the water and gently stir with the brush or toothpick. Lay paper (smaller than the pan) onto the swirled surface and remove immediately, laying it on newspapers to dry.

To Begin

I always begin class by having the children sit in a semicircle in the center of the room, half on chairs, and the rest directly in front of them on the floor. This way they can all see the pictures as I read the story, and the project demonstration that follows which takes place in the middle of the circle. I have the tables ready with all the necessary supplies so the students can go straight to them and begin working as soon as the demonstration is over, but they are not tempted to fiddle with anything instead of listening. I place everything I need to present the lesson–book, demonstration supplies, finished examples–on a large sheet of paper or poster board in the center of the semicircle. Sometimes I cover some portions while I am reading so the students will not anticipate the art lesson before they hear the story.

Before I read the story to the children, I tell them the author and, of course, the illustrator along with any interesting tidbits I may know about either. We always discuss how the illustrations were done. With practice, the students can differentiate between paint, cut paper, pencil drawings, collage and the many other media used by illustrators today, and they love to take a guess even if they do not know. At this time we may discuss other artists who work in the same style or medium, or paint the same subject matter. Usually examples of famous artists' work can be found in art books in the library.

Each class each year seems to have its own unique personality and abilities. The activities suggested in this book can be modified to meet your own class' needs. You know your class best. You may want to simplify an activity by using crayons instead of paint or tracing shapes for those students who may become frustrated when faced with this task. There are also natural breaks in many of the activities so that they can be completed in small segments. The main objective is to challenge every student, but keep the activities joyful, positive experiences for all.

Puss in Boots

*Illustrated by Fred Marcellino, written by Charles Perrault and translated by Malcolm Arthur.
Farrar, Straus and Giroux, 1990.*

Story Summary

The clever cat Puss, sole legacy left to the third and youngest son of the miller, proves his worth through creative skullduggery. As a result, the miller's son gets the king's daughter, the ogre's palace and lives happily ever after. Puss enjoys the improved circumstances and spends his days lazily dozing on soft carpets. He has given up chasing mice–except now and then just for the fun of it!

Illustrations and Comments

The story's an old one, written by Perrault in the very late 1600s. The translation's a good one, but the illustrations by Marcellino are phenomenal. He works in pastel pencils on a medium tone, medium textured beige paper to which he adds lighter and darker values. The artwork is well researched and accurately depicts the costumes and pastoral countryside of seventeenth century France.

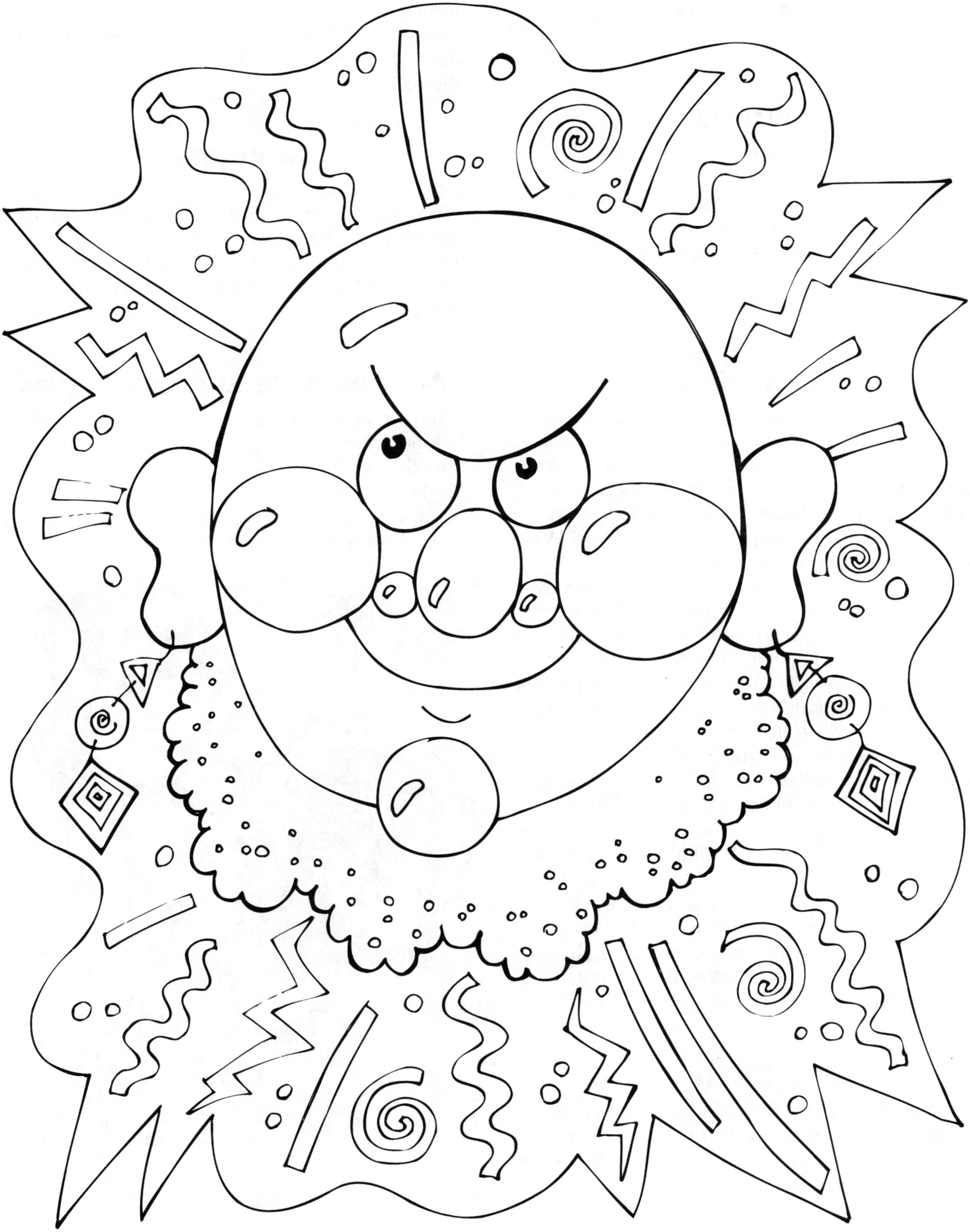

Art Activity

An Ogre's Odd Ability

Materials

beige or grayish construction paper or pastel paper
white chalk and colored chalk or pastels in tones darker than the paper
hair spray or spray fixative (optional)
scissors
string to hang finished art

Directions

After reading the story for enjoyment, turn back to the pages which show the ogre and the animals into which he changes. Have the children think of words that describe the looks of this despicable yet gullible creature. What colors and shapes did the artist use to draw him? What objects does his face remind them of? A sausage? A balloon? A pig? Demonstrate how to draw an ogre's face with round and oval shapes using dark orange or brown chalk–the goofier the better. After all, it is an ogre. Show how to bring out the roundness with white chalk to highlight the bald head, cheeks and nose as shown. Have the children create their own ogre. Be sure to have them add details such as earrings and a collar. When they have completed their ogres, they should cut the edges of their papers in zigzags or waves so that they look like magical "poofs." Ask the children what animal they would turn into if they were ogres, and have them draw those animals on the back of their ogres. Be sure to add the word *Poof!* Show the students how artists "fix" their chalk drawings to prevent smudging by spraying a light coat or two of spray fixative or hair spray.

Display

Punch a hole at the top of each drawing and hang from the ceiling or light fixture with a string so that both sides can be seen as the piece turns gently. Cut one zigzag shape slightly larger than the rest. On one side write *Poof!* in decorative letters and *An Ogre's Odd Ability* on the other.

Related Artists

Compare the costumes of the peasants and the aristocracy in the book to those in the paintings of Hogarth, Chardin, Watteau, Anthony Van Dyck and other French and Dutch masters who painted at the turn of the eighteenth century (1700).

Art Concepts and Techniques

Drawing lighter and darker in chalk on medium tone paper
Blending chalk
Cutting
Drawing
Use of spray to "fix" artwork

Little Red Riding Hood

Illustrated and retold by Trina Schart Hyman. Holiday House, 1983.

Story Summary

This version of the German tale features a young, innocent Red Riding Hood who is waylaid when the villain wolf convinces her to stray from the path to gather wildflowers for her ailing grandmother. The wolf then races ahead, gobbles up Grandmother and takes her place so that he can gobble Red for dessert. Sated by his excellent meal, he falls asleep and his snoring alerts a passing huntsman who slices the wolf's stomach open and releases the frightened pair.

Illustrations and Comments

Trina Schart Hyman was awarded a Caldecott Honor Book award for her charming and detailed illustrations of this story. The students will enjoy picking out the cat that appears on nearly every page as well as the forest creatures, flowers and patterns in small pictures within the borders. There was some controversy when this book came out because the grandmother enjoyed wine.

8

TLC10045 Copyright © Teaching & Learning Company, Carthage, IL 62321

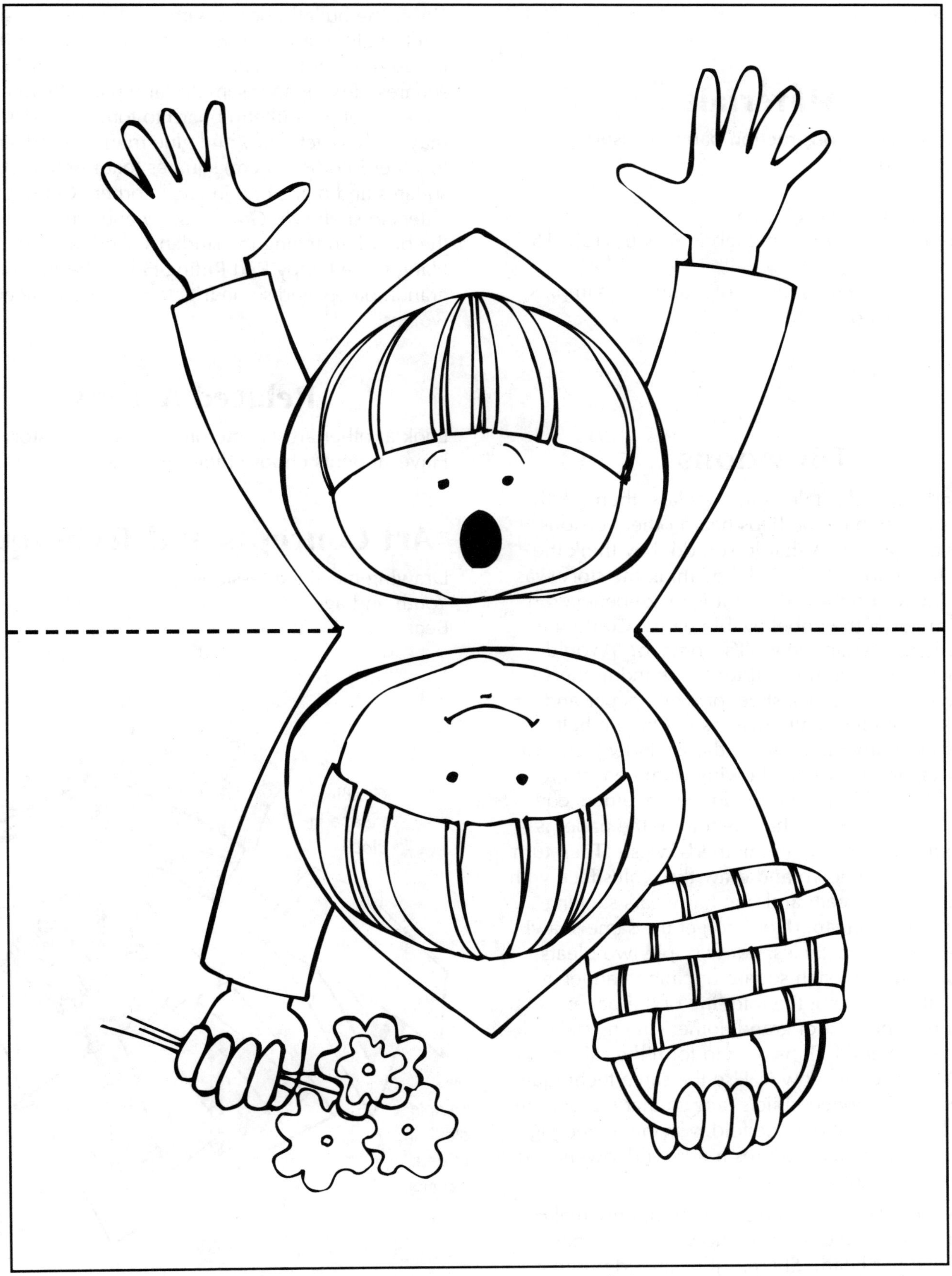

Art Activity

Oh, Grandmother

Materials

white drawing or construction paper measuring 9" x 12" (23 x 30 cm)
crayons
red fabric 6" x 6" (15 x 15 cm)
white or calico print flannel fabric 6" x 6" (15 x 15 cm)
3" or 4" (8 or 10 cm) squares of wallpaper samples
black construction paper
stapler
scissors

Directions

Read and enjoy this tale with the class, then ask the students if they have perhaps heard other versions which vary slightly. What lesson do they think the story is trying to teach? Did they think the story was frightening, or do they realize it is make-believe? Ask them about the unbelievable parts. Could the two really survive in the wolf's stomach? Would they have mistaken the wolf for the grandmother? Now give the students a sheet of white paper and have them fold it in half crosswise. On one half, they should draw the grandmother's kindly face, with spectacles, and gray hair showing from beneath a lacy nightcap. They should add her shoulders covered with her shawl so that the fold of the paper is approximately at the grandmother's waist. Then turn the paper upside down and draw the wolf's face with shiny eyes; large teeth and big, hairy ears sticking out from the nightcap. Don't forget the same shawl and maybe the spectacles. Now staple two pleats along one edge of each square of calico flannel and staple that edge along the fold line of the paper so that it forms the skirt of grandmother's nightgown and, when inverted, flops over to form the skirt of the wolf's borrowed gown. Use the same technique to make a red-hooded child's face so that the bottom of the chin is just above the fold, waving a greeting with one hand which perhaps holds wildflowers and the other hand holds a basket.

Flip the sheet and draw the same child, only make her expression one of fear, as shown, waving her arms above her head. She has just figured out that her sweet grandmother is a wolf! Attach the red piece of fabric along the fold line.

Display

Cover the bulletin board with a solid color or small print of gift wrap or fabric similar to those the illustrator used in her borders. Cut 3" or 4" (8 or 10 cm) squares of wallpaper samples and place them around the edge of the bulletin board to form a border. You may wish to get fancy and glue triangles and squares together into 6" (15 cm) squares that resemble quilt squares and place one in each corner. Cut out black letters to spell *Oh, Grandmother* and attach them to the board arranging the students' work around them. Hang some happy Red Riding Hoods beside their grandmothers and some frightened ones beside the wolves.

Related Artists

Look at other artists' interpretations of the story. Have students choose their favorites.

Art Concepts and Techniques

Drawing facial expressions
Youth and age
Beasts

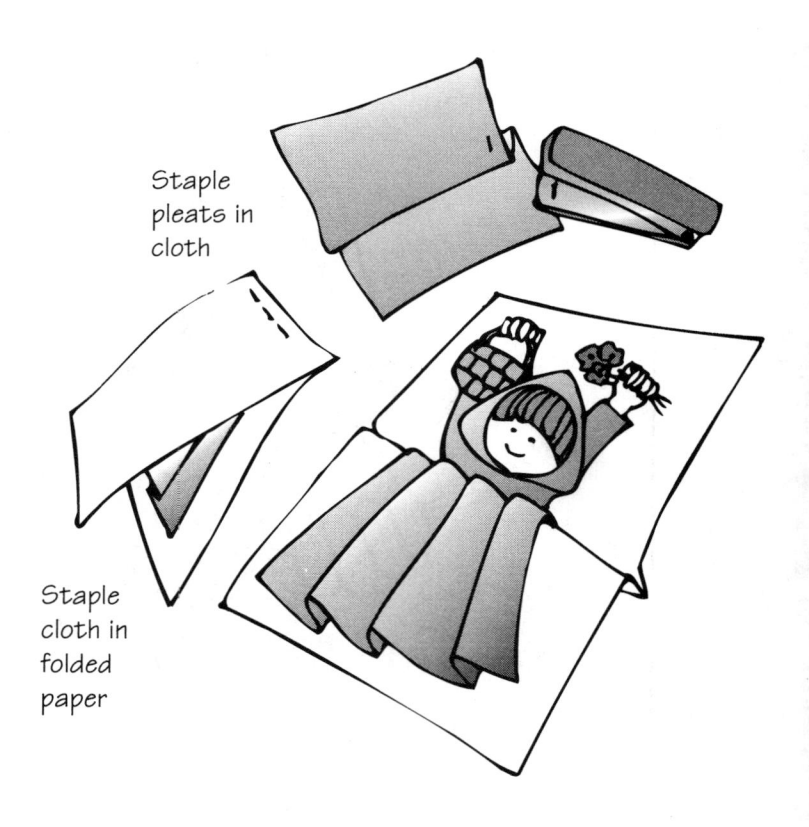

Staple pleats in cloth

Staple cloth in folded paper

Goldilocks and the Three Bears

Illustrated and retold by Jan Brett. G.P. Putnam's Sons, 1987.

Story Summary

The bear family who lives in the woods decide to go for a walk while their porridge cools. While they are gone, Goldilocks visits their cottage and helps herself to the bear's breakfast. She then sits in their chairs and finally falls asleep in small, wee bear's bed. The bears return and are surprised to find her sleeping there, but not as surprised as Goldilocks herself, who dashes away without a backwards glance.

Illustrations and Comments

Jan Brett is a prolific illustrator who cleverly inserts subplots and side stories into the borders of her pictures. In this story, we see Goldilocks exploring the woods in the borders as the bears leave their cottage for their walk. As the bears check out their bowls of porridge, we are reminded that Goldilocks is sleeping upstairs, soon to be discovered. What I like best about this version though is the design of the home of the bears.

Art Activity

It was too HOT!

Materials

colored chalk or pastels
white drawing paper
scissors
newspapers
colored construction paper
stapler

Directions

Read the story through so the children can enjoy it once again, and compare this version with others they may have heard. Discuss the difference between these make-believe animals and real bears in the wild or the zoo. Real bears, except perhaps in the circus, do not wear clothing, live in cottages with chairs and beds and bowls for porridge. Now go back and look more carefully through the illustrations by Jan Brett. If you came across this cottage deep in the woods, how would you know that bears lived here? The beehives to insure an ample supply of honey? The carvings on the door, the lintels and the columns? See how many "beary" items and motifs they can spot on each page. Note the dangling bumblebee tassels on the great, huge bear's clothing; the chairs and beds; the needlepoint cushions; the wallpaper; the teapot and especially the three bowls. Ask the students to imagine what their bowls would look like if they were bears. Have each student fold a sheet of white drawing paper in half crosswise and cut a symmetrical bowl shape as shown. You may have to sketch the lines in pencil for some students, but bowls which the students design themselves are generally more interesting. Details befitting a bear can be added with chalk. Be sure the students work on newspapers so they can design the very edge of their bowl without messing up the table. Now have each student select his favorite color of construction paper and staple the bowl near the bottom edge. As a final touch, use white chalk to draw steam curling up from the bowl, smearing it carefully with the fingers for a realistic effect. After all we know it was very, very HOT!

Display

Cover the bulletin board with white paper. Across the center write *It was too HOT!* Use black chalk for the sentence except for the word *HOT!* Use yellow, orange and red chalk to make the word look like fire. Attach the students' bowls to the board around the title. You may wish to have an early finisher draw the top half of Goldilocks' head and place her at the bottom of the display as if she is peeking up at the porridge bowls.

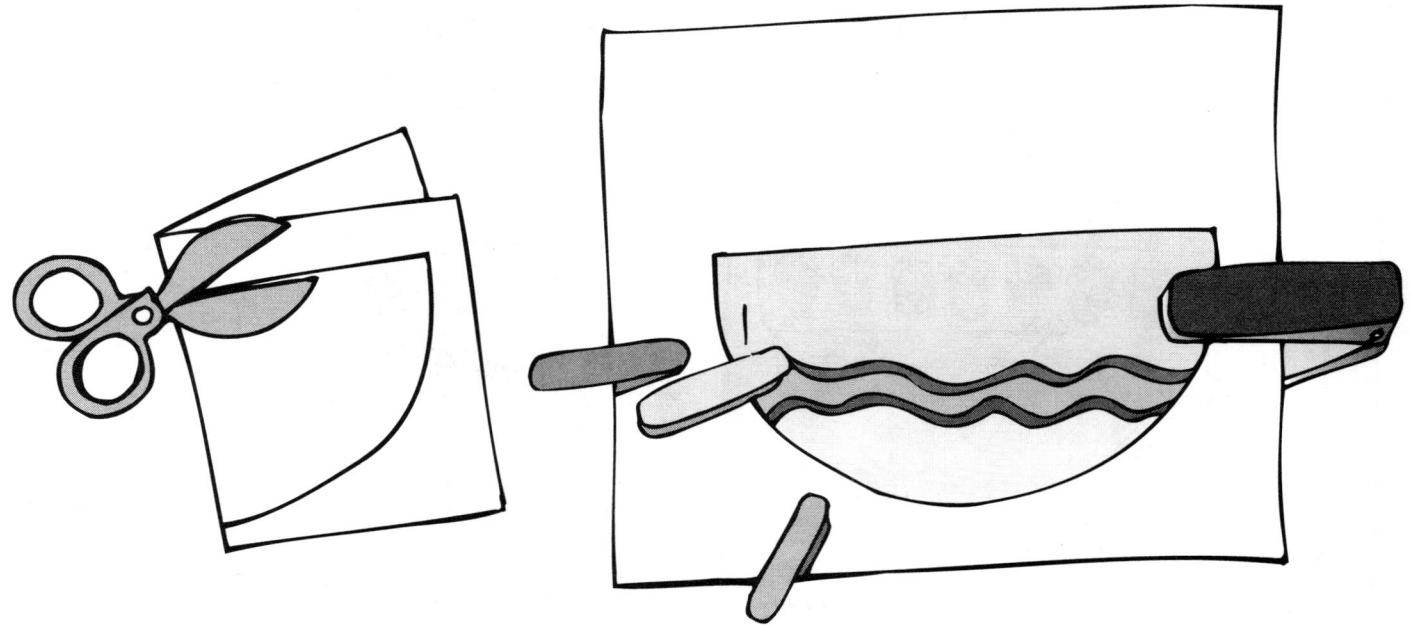

TLC10045 Copyright © Teaching & Learning Company, Carthage, IL 62321

Related Artists

There are many fine artists who design all the different motifs on dinnerware. Assemble a variety of bowls with different designs: rugged stoneware, delicate floral porcelain, ultramodern, old-fashioned, baby bowls, party paper plates. Ask the students to add to the collection. Now ask the students to compare them, and describe the type of person they think would buy and use each type of dinnerware.

Art Concepts and Techniques

Drawing with chalk pastels
Symmetry
Matching design with personality

The Sleeping Beauty

Illustrated and retold by Mercer Mayer. Macmillian, 1984.

Story Summary

It was all due to a misunderstanding. The Blue Faerie (book's spelling) felt slighted because her banquet goblet was not pure gold, so she doomed the king and queen's baby daughter to death. The Star Faerie softened the prophesy from death to death-like sleep, until such time a handsome prince loves her enough to risk his own life to rescue her and awaken her with a kiss.

Illustrations and Comments

This story has both French and German versions, but Mercer Mayer has chosen to fill his illustrations with Celtic motifs, adding braided, intertwining vines not only to the architectural detail, furniture, tapestries and costumes but even to the vines themselves. These illustrations manage to be both crisp and soft at the same time, and the skin of Sleeping Beauty seems to glow from within.

Art Activity

Sleeping Beauty

Materials

white drawing paper measuring 9" x 12" (23 x 30 cm)
crayons or paints
red, rose or pink construction paper
scissors
15" x 1/2" (38 x 1.25 cm) green ribbon or 15 x 1/2" (38 x 1.25 cm) strips torn from green cloth (green with small calico print will work)
stapler
glitter (optional)

Directions

Read the story to the class and compare this version to others they have read. Which elements are universal to all versions? Do the differences matter to the happy ending? Which version do they like best? If each of them were to relate the tale to the class, would they all use exactly the same words? Go back through the pages and point out examples of the braided Celtic details. Have the students point out others. If possible, show an illuminated initial from a medieval manuscript with similar ornamentation. The detail may resemble a student's braided hair. Discuss the thorny rose hedge which grew up wide and thick and tall to envelope the castle and protect the sleeping princess which the prince had to fight his way through in order to rescue her. In these illustrations, Mercer Mayer has even drawn the thorny hedge with a Celtic motif! Now have the students color or paint their favorite part of the story on a sheet of white paper. They may wish to portray Sleeping Beauty sound asleep, or the handsome prince battling the terrible ogre of the enchanted forest. Once they have completed their illustrations and they have dried thoroughly, staple six 15" x 1/2" (38 x 1.25 cm) strips of green cloth (torn to look thorny, not cut) or ribbon across the bottom of the artwork. Then have the students braid and cross and twist the strips so that they appear to be a thick hedge growing up intertwined and covering the scene as shown. Once the students have reached the top of their artwork, staple the strips in place across the top to secure them. Finally, have the students draw three or four roses about 1" (2.5 cm) in diameter, drawing petals in dark red or purple crayon on red, rose or pink paper. Sleeping Beauty is called Briar Rose in the German version of this tale. Cut the roses out and staple them to the cloth strips as if they are growing on the vines. It will appear as if we are peering through a thorny hedge to view the scenes from this favorite fairy tale.

Display

Tear 2" (5 cm) strips of the same green fabric and twist and braid them around the edges of a bulletin board to which the students' illustrations have been stapled. Add a few roses made by using the technique described in the directions, only larger, or staple plastic or silk roses in their place. Enlarge and copy the lettering shown for the title *Sleeping Beauty*. Have early finishers color the illuminated initials, adding a touch of "fairy dust," glitter perhaps, before attaching it to the board.

Related Artists

Look for examples of illuminated manuscripts with richly decorated initial letters such as the Cross Page from the Lindisfarne Gospels created around 700 A.D.

Art Concepts and Techniques

Drawing or painting from imagination
Weaving and braiding
Stapling

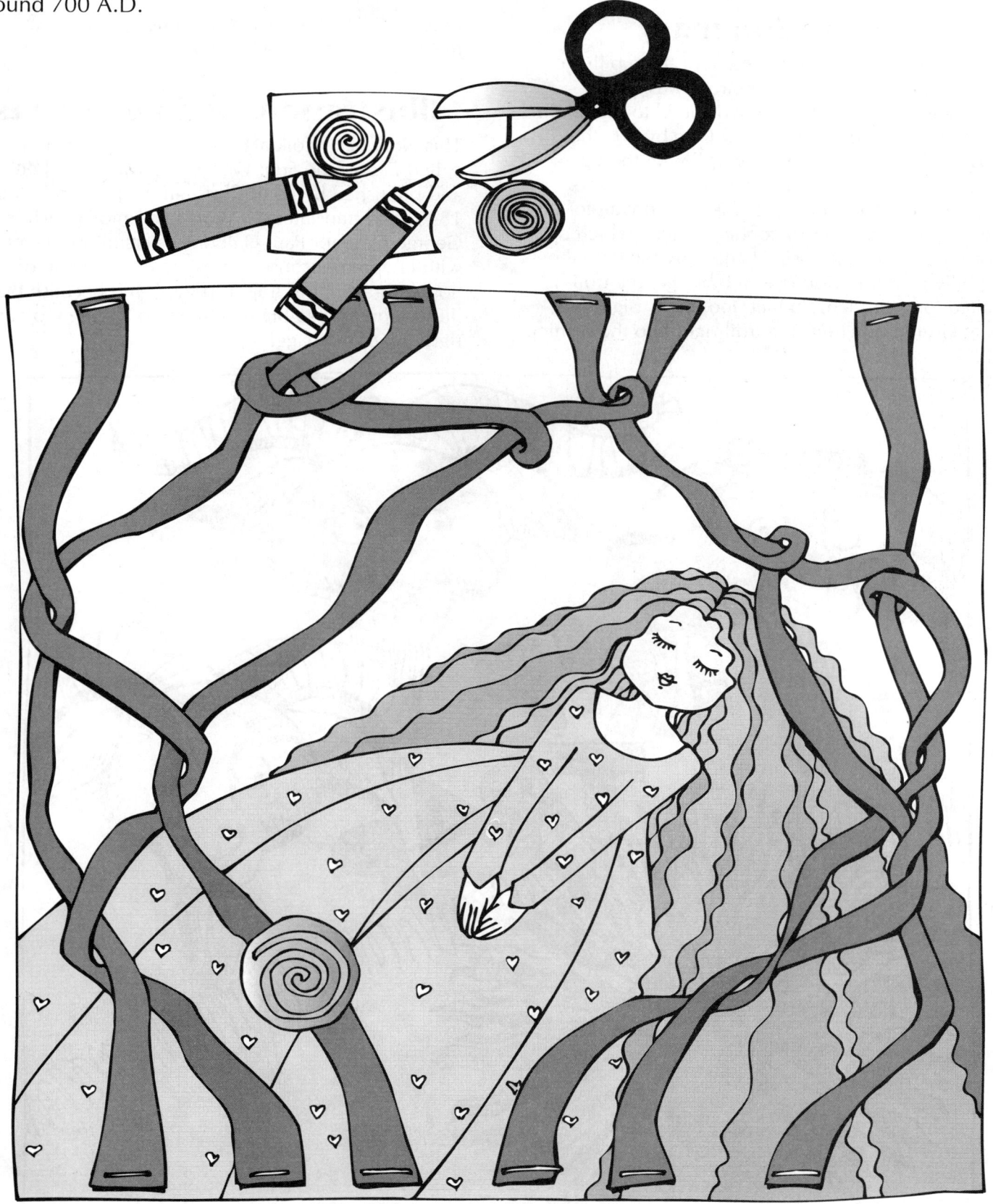

17

TLC10045 Copyright © Teaching & Learning Company, Carthage, IL 62321

The Three Billy Goats Gruff

Illustrated and written by Paul Galdone. Clarion Books, 1973.

Story Summary

The supply of fresh, tender grass for three billy goats, who happened to be named Gruff, was rather skimpy in their valley, so they decided to munch in the meadow across the bridge. One by one they cross and face the mean, ugly troll with the voracious appetite who lives under the bridge. The smallest billy goat convinces the troll to wait for his bigger, juicier brother to gobble, a tactic which also works for the medium-sized goat. By the time the big billy goat trip traps over the bridge, the troll has waited long enough. In fact, too long! Big Billy Goat Gruff easily butts the troll right into the rushing river and continues across the bridge to the grassy meadow and his little brothers.

Illustrations and Comments

This Norwegian folktale was one in a collection called *East of the Sun, West of the Moon*, gathered and published by Peter Christian Asbjornsen in the 1840s and translated 10 years later into English by George Dasent. Paul Galdone's version is a favorite with children because it uses the expected, traditional phrase, "Trip trap, trip trap" and because the illustrations are so big they seem to threaten to come right out of the page!

Art Activity

Trip Trap

Goat 1

Goat 2

Goat 3

Materials

paper plates
assorted paper scraps
crayons or oil crayons
scissors
stapler
yarn for tying masks

Directions

Read this old favorite with great expression, allowing the students to participate if they are familiar with the words. Turn to the beginning of the story and take a closer look at the goats on the first page. Have the students describe their similarities (eyes, noses, beards) and their differences (size, color, shape of horns). Divide the class into groups of four, and assign each group member one of the four characters in the story. Now demonstrate how the students can make goat and troll masks using paper plates and the patterns on the following pages. You may have to sketch the main lines for some of the students, and cut out the eyes as it is difficult for young students to punch through the heavy paper. The billy goats should be colored with lines that follow the way their hair grows on their faces and ears. The ridges on the paper plates will show up as the natural ridges on the goats' horns. Cut slits on each side of the snout and bend it slightly forward to give the students' nose some room. You will need to help the students assemble the masks with a stapler once all the pieces have been colored and cut out. Staple two pieces of heavy yarn, string or shoestring near the eyes to tie the finished masks on. A generous loop of masking tape will affix the beard to the chin of each goat. One student in each group must play the troll. (Or perhaps you'd like to reserve that privilege for yourself.) The construction of the troll's mask also begins with a paper plate using the pattern provided. In this book, the troll's big nose is blue and his eyes are rimmed with dark circles, but artistic license could be taken as the student sees fit. The wild hair is created by tearing long strips of various colors of construction paper, paper bags, wallpaper, even newspaper and gluing or stapling them at one end to the outside rim of the plate, working inward with additional rows until only the nose and dark circles around the eyes show. Staple yarn in the same fashion as the goat masks.

Display

Once the masks are completed, assembled and dried, the students can use them while they practice their dramatic skills by retelling the story to their classmates, other classes or their parents. They can also be arranged on a bulletin board that has been covered with green paper which early finishers have fringed along the top side so that it resembles grass. Place the troll at the bottom, then the words *The grass is always greener* or *Trip Trap* above them and finally, the Gruff family of goats.

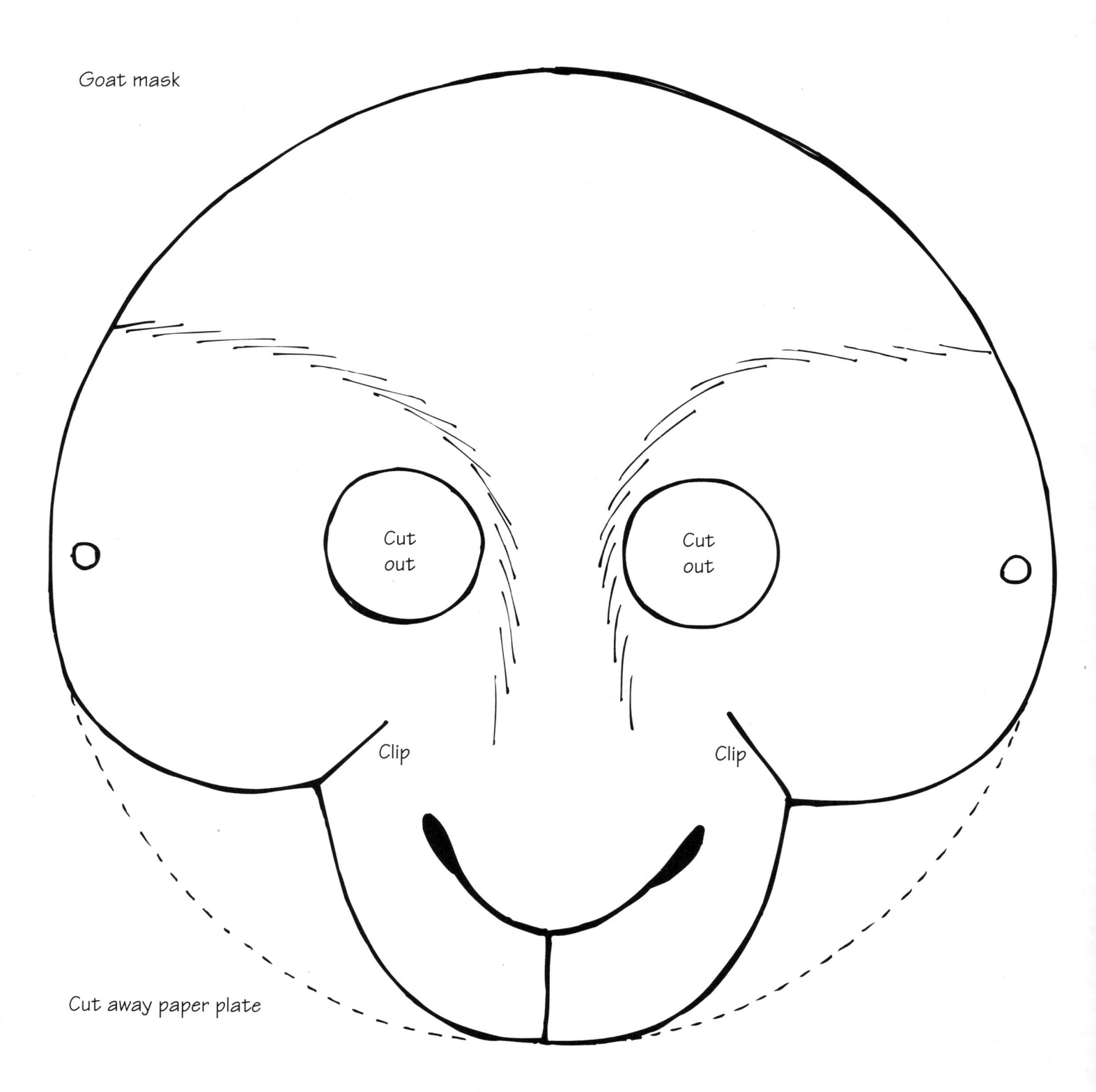

Goat mask

Cut out

Cut out

Clip

Clip

Cut away paper plate

20

TLC10045 Copyright © Teaching & Learning Company, Carthage, IL 62321

Troll mask

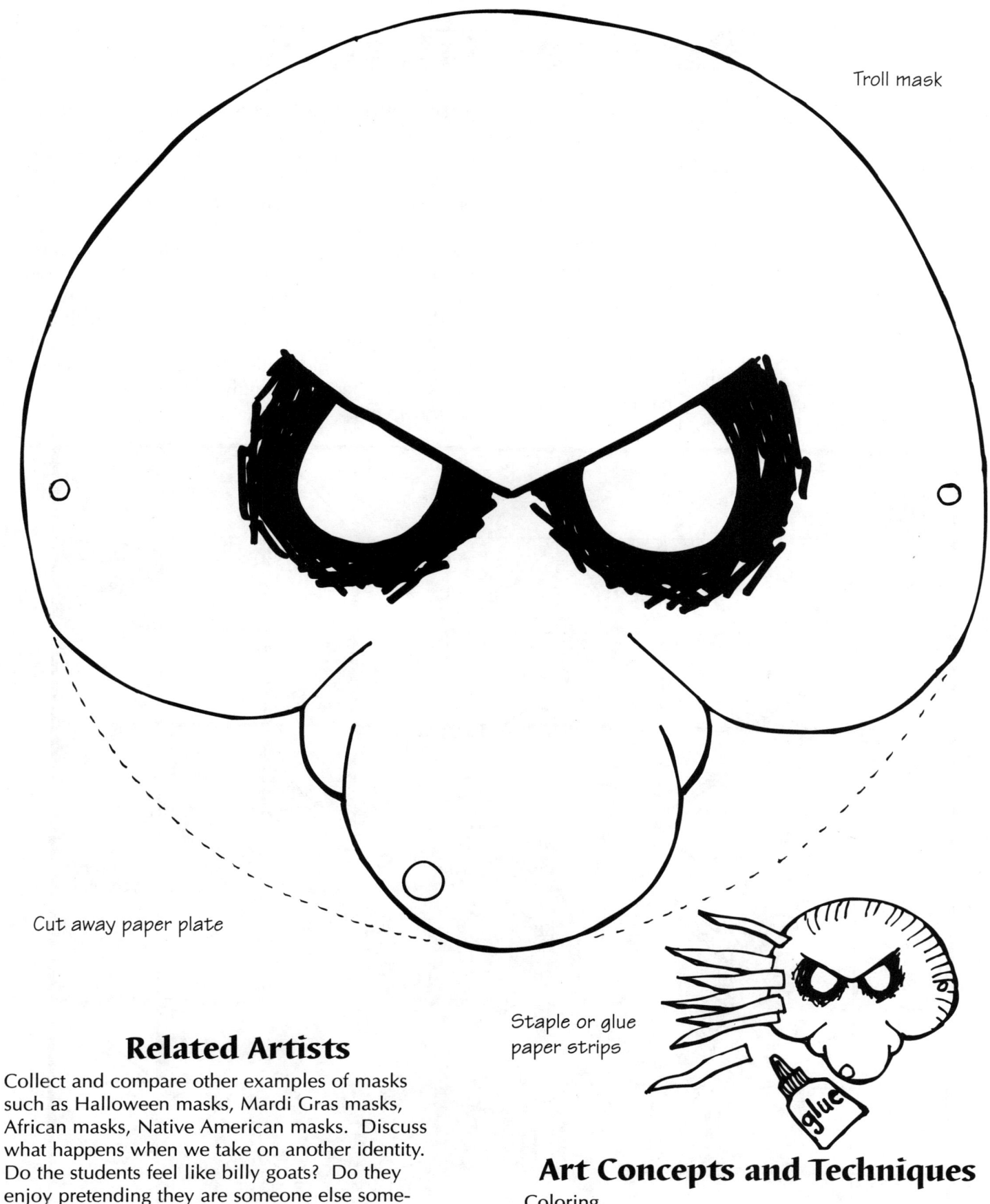

Cut away paper plate

Staple or glue paper strips

Related Artists
Collect and compare other examples of masks such as Halloween masks, Mardi Gras masks, African masks, Native American masks. Discuss what happens when we take on another identity. Do the students feel like billy goats? Do they enjoy pretending they are someone else sometimes?

Art Concepts and Techniques
Coloring
Cutting
Mask-making

21

Rumpelstiltskin

Illustrated and retold by Paul O. Zelinsky and originally collected by the Brothers Grimm. E.P. Dutton, 1986.

Story Summary

When a foolish miller boasts to the king that his beautiful daughter can spin straw into gold, the king shuts her in a castle room full of straw and a spinning wheel and threatens to put her to death if she does not prove her father's boast. The maiden is distraught until a little man appears and, in return for her necklace, completes the task for her. But the greedy king is not satisfied, and the second night the maiden must trade her ring for the little man's services. On the third night, when she has nothing left to give the little man, but since the king has promised to marry her, in desperation she promises her firstborn child. One year later, when the maiden, now queen, has a small son and has all but forgotten her promise, the little man appears and demands the child. She pleads so pitifully that he relents, if and only if she can guess his name in three days. Though she guesses every name she can think of, she fails until she sends her servant through the forest to spy on him and overhears him singing out his name. This information the servant reports to her queen who then successfully guesses and so may keep her child.

Illustrations and Comments

Zelinsky's beautiful illustrations done in the style typical of the late Middle Ages or early Renaissance seem to glow just as the golden spools that Rumpelstiltskin spins shine out from where they lie amongst the straw. The first known written form of this tale was by the Grimm brothers and showed up in 1808 to be published in a collection in 1812. The original story underwent several alterations in years since. Paul O. Zelinsky combined the best of all the versions and added a few touches of his own.

Art Activity

What's my name?

Materials

stiff paper or oaktag measuring 9" (23 cm) square and divided into a grid of 3" (8 cm) squares
3" (8 cm) squares in assorted colors of construction paper or any decorative paper that resembles stone or marbleized paper (see directions in recipes section on page 2)
sheets of yellow or gold paper
actual pieces of straw or long slivers of orange or tan paper
gold foil scraps
royal blue or purple paper
scissors
glue
stapler

Directions

Read and enjoy the story and have the students compare it with other versions they may have read. Ask the students their opinions of the characters in the story–the miller, his daughter, the king, Rumpelstiltskin. Which were good? Which were bad? This story provides a good opportunity to explore the complexities of right and wrong. I have always felt sorry for the little guy in this fairy tale! Anyway, after the story has been discussed, look back through the illustrations and have students note the elaborate tile designs on the floor of each room. They will be able to spot many examples of squares, triangles, diamonds and circles in contrasting colors. Ask the students if they can think of examples of tiles they have noticed–the floors and walls of their kitchens or the restroom at school, even their favorite quilt may have tile-like pieces. Challenge them to design a tile floor of their own on a 9" (23 cm) square of paper. You may have to lightly mark grid lines for the students before you begin. This can be done easily by cutting a 9" x 3" (23 x 8 cm) strip of stiff paper or oaktag and using it as a straightedge. Line it up against one side of the 9" square as shown and draw a line. Rotate the square one quarter turn and draw another line. Repeat on all four sides. Give the students 3" (8 cm) squares of paper in assorted colors to glue onto their larger square. They may simply glue them down as they are; cut some into triangles, circles or diamonds; or create a shape of their own, depending on their abilities. Be sure to have them lay out their design and move pieces around until they are satisfied with it before they begin gluing.

9" x 9" square
9" x 3" oaktag template

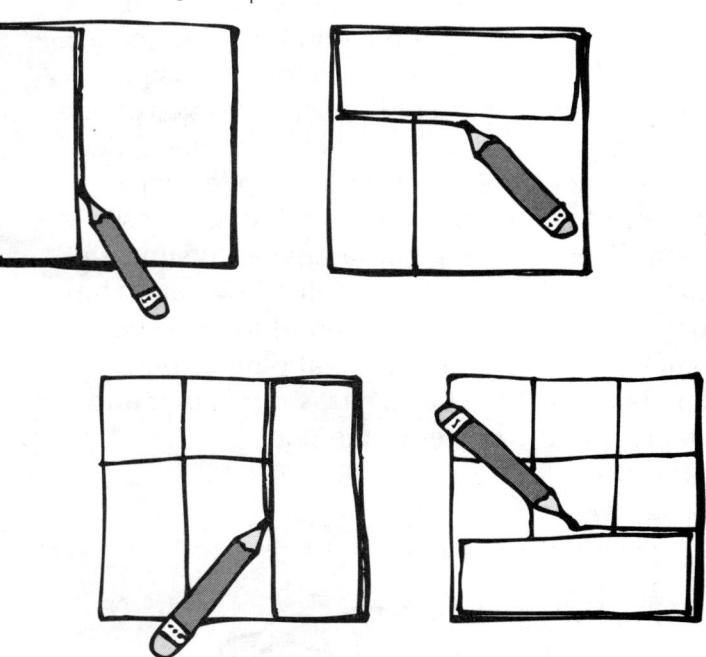

TLC10045 Copyright © Teaching & Learning Company, Carthage, IL 62321

23

Display

When the students' artwork has dried completely, use it to tile a bulletin board, placing the squares so that the edges touch. Use a few sheets of yellow or gold paper to fashion a pile and attach it to the center bottom of the "tiled" bulletin board. Onto half of the pile, staple pieces of actual straw, if available, or cut some long slivers of orange or tan paper to simulate straw. Add scraps of gold foil (chocolate wrappers work well for this purpose) to the other half of the pile. Cut out royal blue or purple letters to spell the title *What's my name?* and staple it in the center of the pile.

Related Artists

Look in any art history book to find paintings of the late Middle Ages and the early Renaissance (around 1400-1450) and compare the costumes, castles and landscapes to the illustrations in the book. I believe Zelinsky's castle to be the same castle painted in 1413-16 by the Limbourg Brothers in the work entitled, *October* from *Les Tres Riches Heures du Duc de Berry*. If there is a spinner in your area, invite her to demonstrate the process in your classroom. Ask her if she is able to turn straw into gold as Rumpelstiltskin did!

Art Concepts and Techniques

Geometric shaped designs
Cutting
Gluing

25

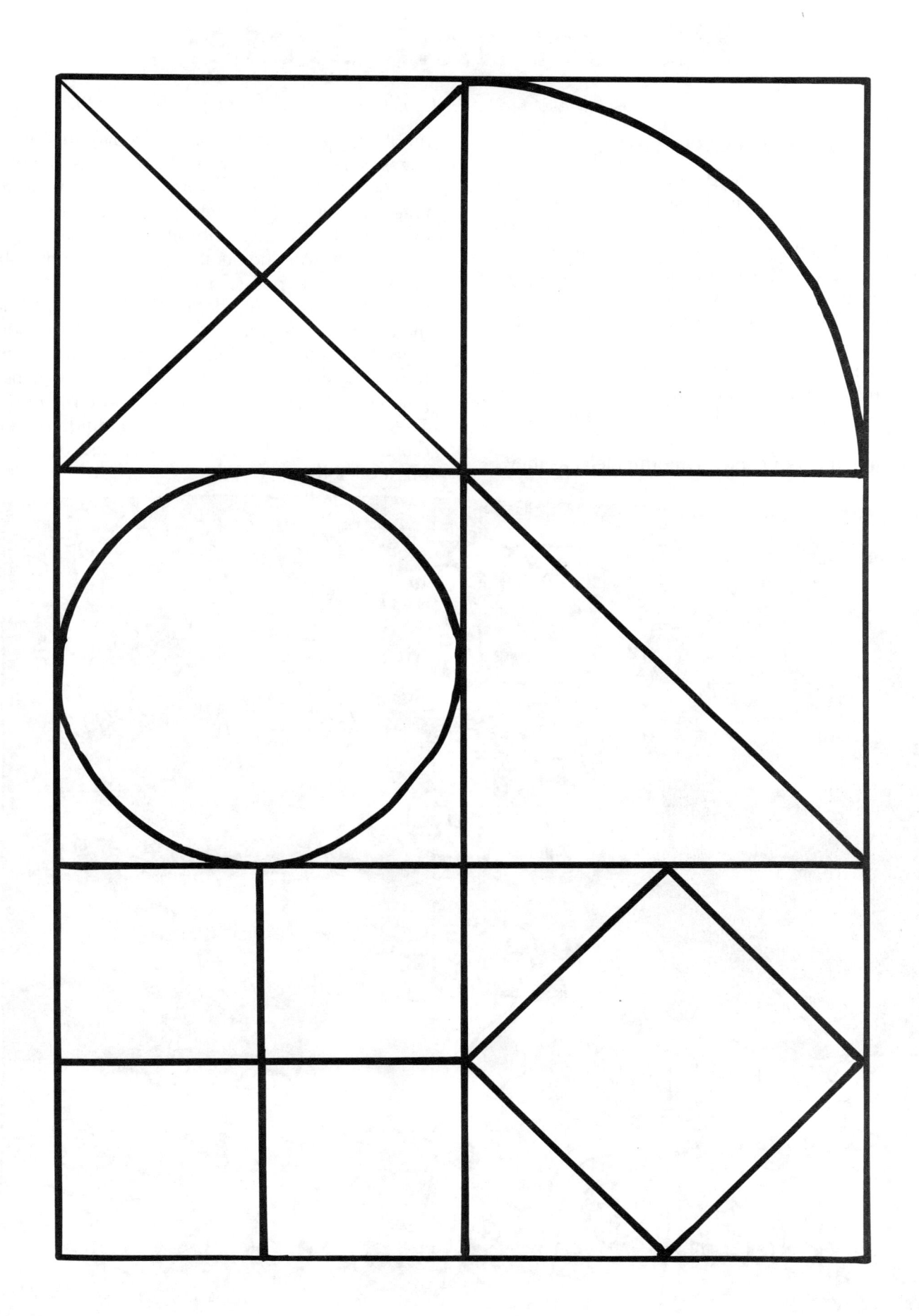

Hansel and Gretel

Illustrated and retold by James Marshall. Dial Books for Young Children, 1990.

Story Summary

The poor woodcutter's greedy wife, fearful that there will not be enough food for herself, convinces her husband to take his two darling children, Hansel and Gretel, deep into the woods and leave them there. Clever Hansel collects small white pebbles and drops them along the path so the two children can find their way back. More determined than ever to rid herself of the children, the mother bolts the door so that Hansel cannot get more stones for their second trip into the woods. He must drop bread crumbs instead, which the hungry forest birds eat. Lost in the woods, they wander until they spy a cottage made entirely of candy. Unfortunately, as they nibble away, the home owner, an overdressed witch, cages Hansel for a later meal and forces Gretel to slave over the stove, cooking enormous meals to fatten him up. But the resourceful pair are not daunted. First Hansel substitutes a chicken bone for his finger to fool the nearly blind witch when she checks his plumpness. Then Gretel saves the day by tricking the witch into demonstrating how to check the oven's temperature. Gretel seizes the opportunity to shove the witch into the hot oven and slams the door. The two children discover boxes of gems and gold coins when they explore the witch's house. They return home with the loot and find, to their delight, that their father's wife has died. From then on, life is bliss.

Illustrations and Comments

James Marshall's illustrations are as funny as his words. The two together make quite an entertaining version for adults as well as children, that is not so scary as this story could be. Indeed, not so frightening as it was when originally published by the Brothers Grimm.

Art Activity
Nibble, Nibble

Materials
black and red construction paper
tempera paint
Styrofoam™ trays
brushes and small sponges
white paper
crayons or Craypas™
brown paper bag
scissors
glue
real candies (optional)

Directions
Enjoy this humorous tale with the class and take some time to compare it to other versions the students may have heard. Were they less frightened by this one? What made it less scary? Which words? Which pictures? Now go back through the book and take a closer look at the forest. How many different colors of green does the illustrator use to paint all the different trees? Look outside the window and note the varying shades that occur in real life. A slight variation of this activity is to have students first make brown by mixing orange and black tempera poured into one Styrofoam™ tray and use a brush to paint several vertical stripes on their black paper to represent tree trunks. Add foliage on these tree trunks and the forest floor using the method described above. When paintings dry, have students use brown paper and Craypas™ to add a mini gingerbread house to each deep, dark forest scene. Give each student a sheet of black construction paper to represent the darkness, and have them fill it with as many different colors of foliage as they can. Pour yellow, green and a little black, white and red tempera into large, shallow Styrofoam™ trays and mix the colors in different proportions to make every shade of green imaginable. Dab the newly invented shades of green onto the black paper with bits of sponges to create the effect of foliage in the forest. Now ask the children what is their favorite candy that they would like to see on a gingerbread house. Have them draw, color and cut out peppermint sticks, M & M's™, candy canes, cookies, etc. Cut a house shape from a brown paper bag and glue on a white roof cut from paper or Styrofoam™ (adds depth). Have the students glue on their colorful candies to decorate the witch's cottage. You may even wish to hot-glue a few real pieces of candy to the masterpiece!

Sponge-print green foliage

Mix brown to paint trunks

Display

Reserve a few of the students' confections and the real ones, and glue them to bright red letters that spell the title *Nibble, Nibble*. When the forest foliage paintings have dried, attach them to the bulletin board, overlapping them slightly so that one big forest is created. Add the gingerbread house to the scene and the red letters across the top.

Art Concepts and Techniques

Color mixing
Drawing
Coloring
Cutting

Related Artists

Compare the greens the students have mixed in their paintings to the many greens in paintings such as, *The Peaceable Kingdom* by Henri Rousseau.

Gingerbread house pattern

Reduce or enlarge as needed, and add confections

Jack and the Beanstalk

Illustrated and retold by Steven Kellogg. Morrow Junior Books, 1991.

Story Summary

Jack is asked by his poor old widowed mother to trade in Milky-white the cow, when she no longer gives milk, but the magic beans he returns with were not what she had in mind. Furious, she tosses them out the window, and by the next morning there is a beanstalk reaching up to the sky. Jack cannot resist climbing it to find a great but tall ogre's house. The ogre's wife hides him where he can witness the ogre counting bags of gold, which Jack makes off with when the ogre dozes. When the gold runs out, he returns to steal the hen who lays golden eggs, and finally, a magic harp. But as Jack grabs the harp, it calls out to its master and wakes him. The ogre chases Jack down the beanstalk, but Jack is quick enough to chop down the beanstalk, and the ogre "fell down and broke his crown and the beanstalk came tumbling after," as Kellogg puts it!

Illustrations and Comments

Though this story first appeared in the volume, *English Folktales* edited and adapted for children by Joseph Jacobs in 1889, he claims to have first heard it in Australia in the 1860s. Steven Kellogg's illustrations are about as colorful as they can be. Even Milky-white the cow is painted in soft shades of the rainbow. The beanstalk and the sky seem alive as Jack makes his first foray into the ogre's kingdom. The ogre is so wonderfully wicked that we feel he deserves all he gets from Jack, but just in case we have the slightest pity for the wretch, Kellogg illustrates how he came by his treasures on the front endpaper and the title pages. The story continues after "the end" on the back endpaper where we glimpse the happily ever after.

Art Activity

Fe Fi Fo Fum

Materials

dried beans, such as limas
small containers such as Styrofoam™ cups
potting soil
cooked dough (recipe on page 2)
clothespins
crayons or markers
pencils
sticks
pipe cleaners
paper scraps
yarn

Poke drain holes in bottom

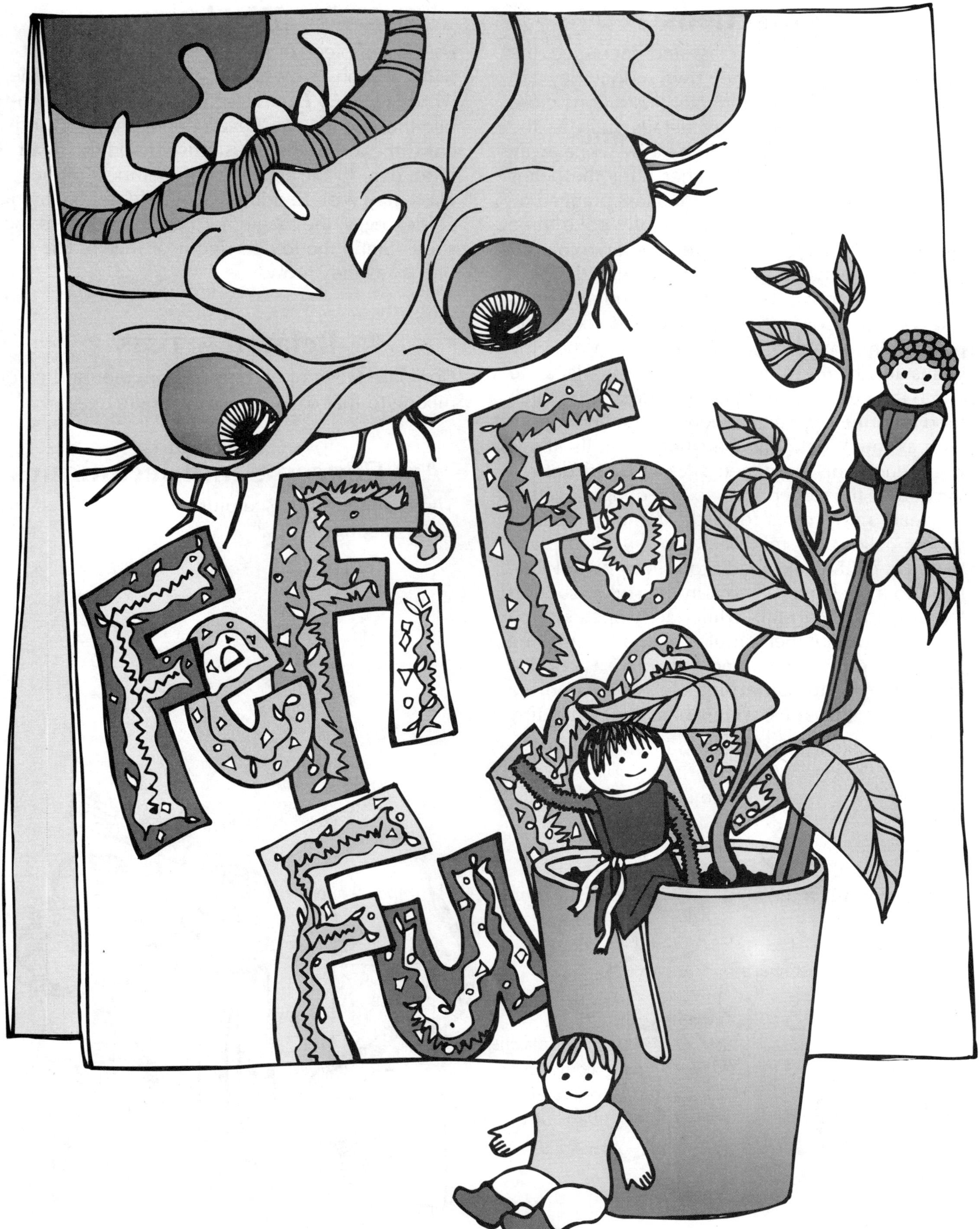
Fe Fi Fo Fum

Directions

Share the story with the class and encourage the students to reread it on their own so that they can take time to study the intricate illustrations close up. We can all see many details such as the funny-looking old man leading Milky-white away in the distance as Jack's mother hurls the beans out the window. Now have the class plant some magic beans of their own. Carefully poke three small holes in the bottom of the Styrofoam™ cups with a pencil and fill them with potting soil. Place three (or five) beans into the soil and press a layer of dirt over them. Water the seeds and place them on a tray in a sunny spot. When the beanstalks begin to grow, make a tiny "Jack" to climb the beanstalk from cooked dough to which food coloring has been added. Pinch and form it with as much detail as the students' skills allow. Use pencils or sharpened sticks to add details. Encourage the students to mix the dough together to create new colors for Jack's tunic, pants and shoes. Allow the mini Jacks to dry, then place them by each stalk, ready to climb, or hot-glue them to a stick and place it in the soil to support the growing beanstalk while Jack appears to be climbing it. Another simpler method of making Jack is to draw a face and hair onto a wooden clothespin, wrap half a pipe cleaner around the "body" for the arms, and clothe him with tiny scraps of paper as shown.

Display

Fold a stiff piece of paper or poster board so it will stand on its own, and on one half write the words *Fe Fi Fo Fum.* Use many colors to decorate these letters, as Steven Kellogg would, and enlist the aid of the class artist to add the head of an ogre to the sign. Other members of the class may wish to add bags of gold, a hen laying golden eggs, the magic harp or characters in the story. Stand the folded sign near the "magic beans" as they grow.

Related Artists

Compare Steven Kellogg's use of color and color mixing to that of Vincent Van Gogh.

Art Concepts and Techniques

Three-dimensional sculpturing
Color mixing

Three Little Pigs and the Big Bad Wolf

Illustrated and retold by Glen Rounds. Holiday House, 1992.

Story Summary

It's not that she doesn't love them, but it is time they made homes for themselves. So the three little pigs left their mother and set out into the world. The first pig opted for a straw home; the second made his from sticks, but the third chose a sturdy brick edifice. When the wolf huffed and puffed at the straw and stick houses, down they came. The pigs were done for, but the bricks withstood the force, and the wolf was forced to resort to trickery if he wanted this third pig for dinner. He arranged to show the pig a field of turnips at six, but the clever pig slipped out at five and was safely home, munching the tender morsels when the wolf arrived. The wolf, more determined than ever, then invited the pig to the fair at three. Once again, the pig attended early. That was the last straw! The furious wolf decided to gain entrance through the chimney, but the pig had a huge pot of boiling soup on the fire, into which the wolf plunged, adding protein to the pig's diet that night.

Illustrations and Comments

This is another English tale from the collection by folklorist Joseph Jacobs and one that very young children enjoy. Glen Round's loose illustrations appear to have been painted in India ink with a dry brush technique and worked back into with pastels or oil pastels, sometimes smeared, once the ink has dried. The result is fresh and spontaneous.

Art Activity

Three's a Magic Number

Materials

- lightweight pink paper such as 8 1/2" x 11" (22 x 28 cm)
- copy paper
- stiff paper or oaktag
- scissors
- crayons
- glue or staples
- white or colored construction paper measuring 9" x 12" (23 x 30 cm)

Pig pattern

Pig tail

Directions

Enjoy the story with the class. Encourage the students to join in when they know the words, and discuss how this version is similar to and different from others they may have heard. Ask the students to name all the stories they can think of which have threes: three bears, three billy goats, three wishes, three trips up the beanstalk, three nights to guess a name . . . Explain that many fairy tales include this number of things. Why do they think so? This repetition helps us to know what to expect while it builds our anticipation. Now have the students engage in a bit of repetition themselves by cutting out three little pigs. Fold a sheet of thin pink paper accordion fashion five times so that there are six sides each measuring 1 1/2" to 2" (4 to 5 cm) in width. Cut all six thicknesses at once to make three pigs holding hands as shown. You may need to make a pattern from stiff paper or oaktag and trace it or have each student trace his own, depending on the age and skill level of your class. Once the three little pigs have been cut out, details such as eyes, snouts, ears and even clothing can be added. Cut three thin strips from the scraps and curl them around a pencil or crayon to make curly tails. Glue or staple them in place on the back of each pig. On a separate sheet of paper, have each student design the background for his pigs. They may wish to add three homes of straw, sticks and bricks, or the wolf lurking behind a tree or a field of turnips. Staple or glue the pigs to the backgrounds.

Display

Cover the bulletin board with a solid color of paper. White, if the students have worked on colored paper, and colored if they have drawn their pigs' backgrounds on white. Cut a large numeral 3 from several sheets of pink paper pieced together, and outline it and the background with other bright colors. All over the three, write the students' responses to the question of "threes" that you asked them during the discussion, such as "The Three Billy Goats Gruff," "Bears," "Blind Mice" and so on. Attach the three in the center of the board with the students' pigs surrounding it.

Related Artists

Pigs can be rather cute. Collect some photographs of pigs and as many picture books with pigs and other pigs in the art as possible. Have the students compare these for individual style and variations from reality (artistic license!)

Art Concepts and Techniques

Repetition
Symmetry
Drawing
Cutting

Backgrounds

The Gingerbread Man

Illustrated by Megan Lloyd and retold by Eric A. Kimmel. Holiday House, 1993.

Story Summary

Just as the old woman and her husband finished putting the last peppermint button on the Gingerbread Man, he leaped off the table and ran out the door. The couple chased him, as did the sow, the dog, the horse and the cow. When the Gingerbread Man met the clever fox at the riverbank, the fox offered to help him cross if he would only hop on his tail. As the water rose, the fox persuaded the Gingerbread Man to move to his back, his head and finally, his snout, at which time he became the fox's lunch.

Illustrations and Comments

This story comes in many versions from all around the world. This one, illustrated by Megan Lloyd, is particularly lighthearted. The drawings are sunny and simple. It is interesting to note that the artist draws in closer to the fox, just as the fox is luring the Gingerbread Man closer and closer to his choppers.

Art Activity

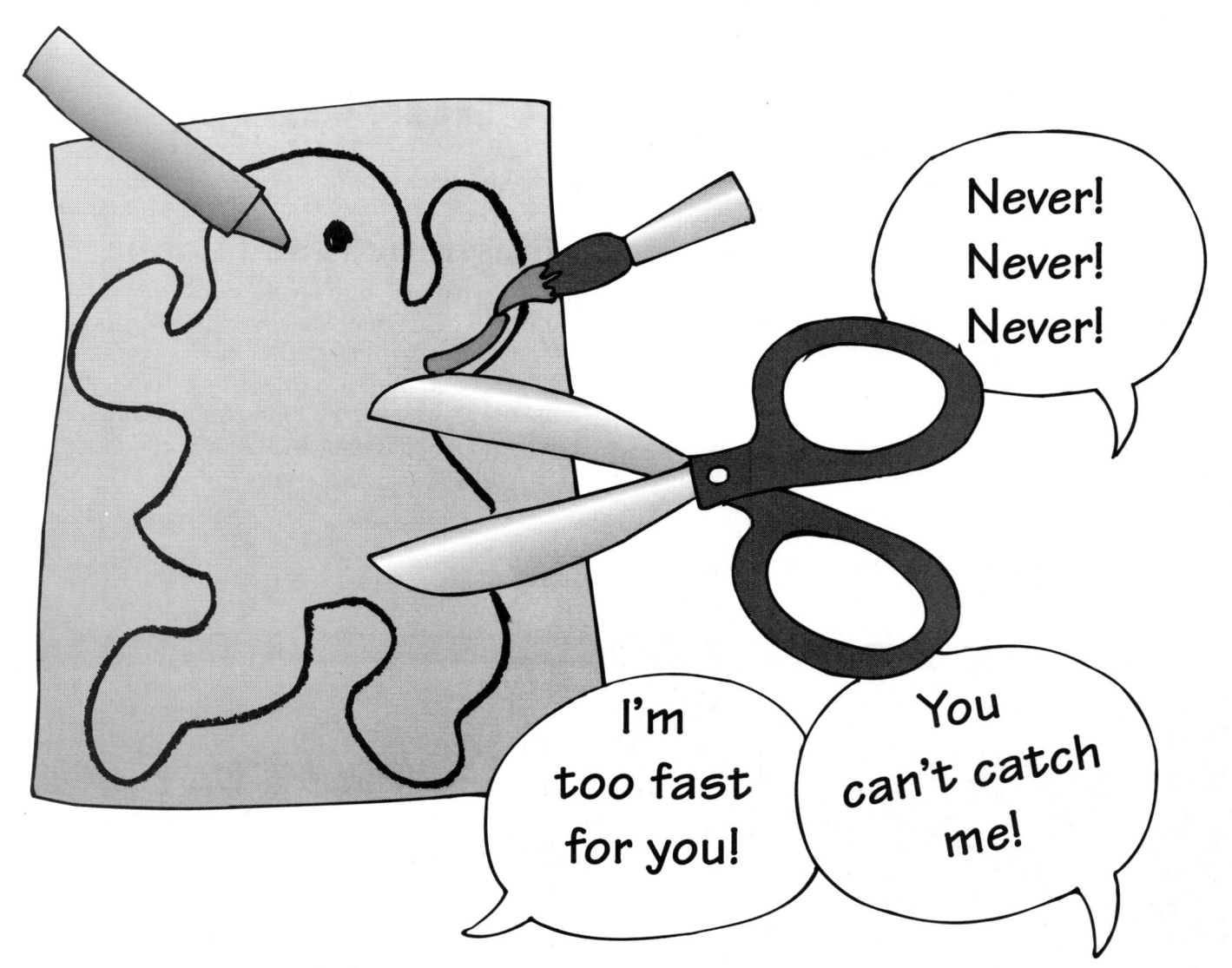

RUN, RUN, RUN

Materials

aluminum foil
brown paper (bags)
crayons
white tempera paint
small brushes
scissors
white paper
stapler

Directions

Enjoy the story with the children and ask them to compare this version of the story to others they may have heard. The author, Eric A. Kimmel, makes sure we are not dismayed at the Gingerbread Man's demise by informing us that he returns whenever gingerbread is baked.

Turning to the last page we see a baking sheet of fresh cookies. Perhaps the Gingerbread Man was a bit too fresh! Ask the students if they think he probably should not have been such a smarty pants! Give each student a piece of brown paper to make a Gingerbread Man. Show them how to make a simple outline and "raisin" eyes with black crayon. They may wish to make men or women or have them running and jumping as they are in the final illustration. Add details with white tempera paint "icing," and cut the figures out when they have dried completely. Next give the students a piece of aluminum foil 6" to 8" (15 to 20 cm) larger than the Gingerbread people and have them fold up the edges to form a lip like a baking sheet. Staple the Gingerbread people to the foil baking sheets. As a final touch, have each student cut out a speech balloon and write in it something that a smarty pants like their characters would but shouldn't say! Staple this to the people.

TLC10045 Copyright © Teaching & Learning Company, Carthage, IL 62321

Display

Cover the bulletin board with a bright blue background. Add red and white candy-striped letters that spell *RUN, RUN, RUN*. Attach the foil baking sheets, with cookies and quips attractively beneath.

Related Artists

To see a flattened cookie figure which should be stiff move and twist as if alive is like Salvador Dali's dripping watches. It is a surprise to our accepted notion of the world. Show the students examples of his paintings and see if they notice a similarity.

Art Concepts and Techniques

Cutting
Painting
Figure proportions
Forming and folding

Double fold foil along dotted lines, crimp corners together to make baking sheet

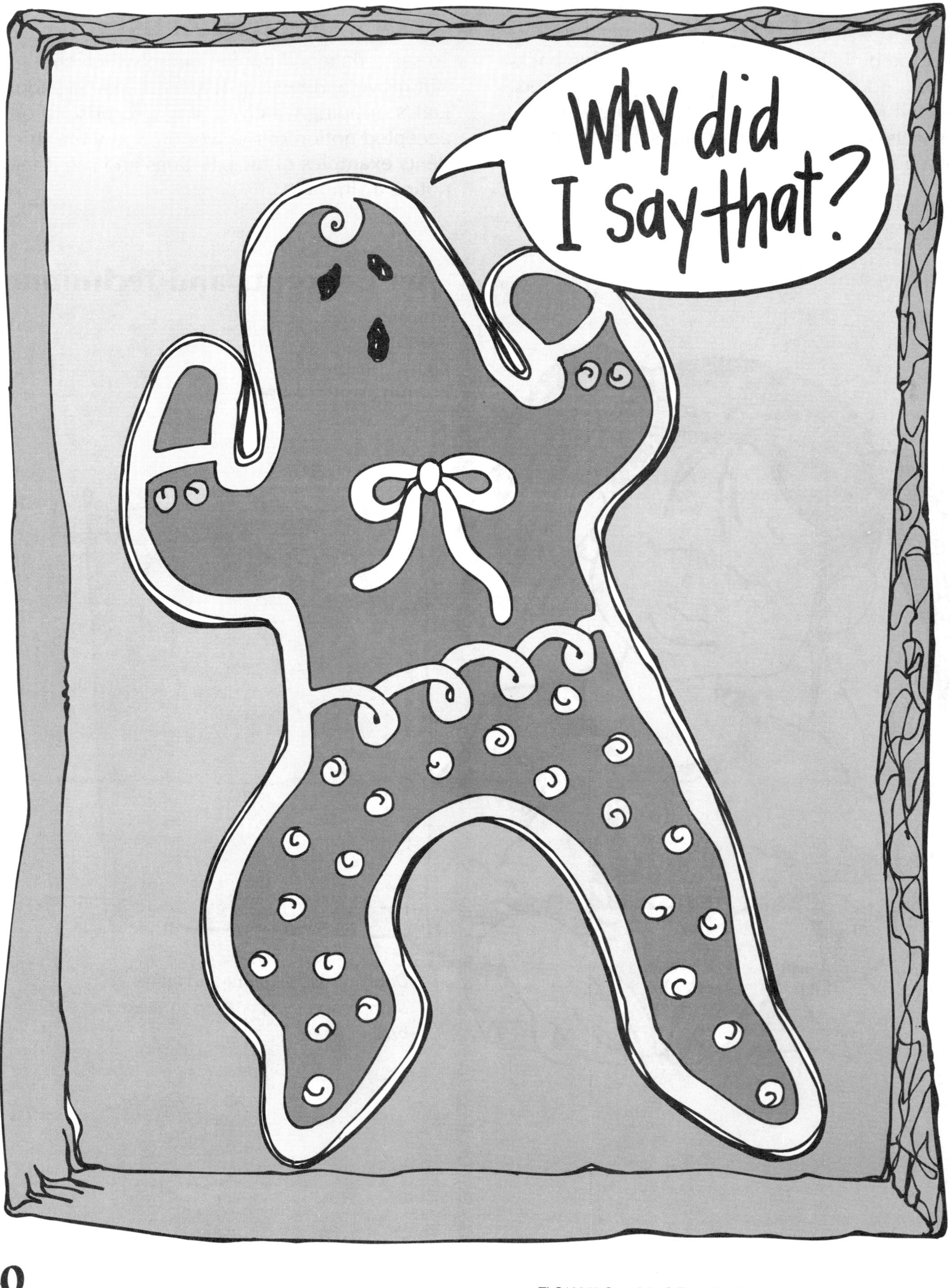
Why did I say that?

Strega Nona

Illustrated and retold by Tomie de Paola. Prentice-Hall, 1975.

Story Summary

Strega Nona or "Grandma Witch" was getting old. So she hired Big Anthony to work for her around the house. One evening he overheard Strega Nona singing over her magic pasta pot and saw that the chant produced steaming hot pasta. Unfortunately, he doesn't stay around long enough to see how she stops the magic. When Strega Nona leaves for the day to visit her friend, she warns him not to touch the pasta pot, but he wants to impress the villagers who laughed at him, so he chants over the pot and it begins to product pasta. All the villagers eat their fill and Anthony is a hero, that is, until the pasta starts overflowing the pot, pours all over the floor, out the door, down the road and threatens to cover the town and its folk, who are running frantically to keep ahead of it. Strega Nona arrives just in time to stop the pasta, save the town and make Big Anthony pay for his mistake–he had to eat all the pasta.

Illustrations and Comments

This tale comes to us from Italy, though there are versions from Germany, Japan and even India. In each, a magic object, misused, leads to big trouble, but it is a simple, gentle story–no one dies or gets gobbled up, or cursed by an evil force. Tomie de Paola's illustrations are wonderful as always, but they are also deceptively simple with many subtleties of gentle color and expression.

Art Activity

Pasta

Materials

white drawing paper
black and white crayons
watercolors
brushes
brown paper for bulletin board or display area

Directions

Share the story with the class and discuss Big Anthony's behavior. Did they know he would do what he did? Why did he do it? Was he showing off? Would the students have been tempted to do the same? Do they think that Strega Nona's punishment was fair? Now take a closer look at the illustrations, and ask the class if they can figure out how Tomie de Paola made them. First he drew the pictures with a dark crayon; then he painted them in with watercolor washes (a little paint and a lot of water). The waxy crayon will not smear because it resists the watercolor. Have the students use a dark crayon to draw the magic pasta pot and Big Anthony beside it, looking worried. Then switch to a white crayon and draw piles of pasta bubbling out of the pot and all over the page. The pasta, drawn with white on white, will not show up yet. Now have the students paint Big Anthony and the pot with watercolor washes. And watch the oodles of noodles magically appear when they begin painting the background.

Display

Measure a large sheet of brown paper to fit the dimensions of the bulletin board or fit several pieces together. Across the top 8" (20 cm), draw tile roofs and arches that resemble the town of Calabria with a dark crayon. In the middle five arches, use a white crayon to write the letters *PASTA*. Invite early finishers to paint the tiles rusty pink shades with watercolor and the archways darker blue or purple so that the word shows up. The students may even want to add a few cobblestones at the bottom. When the paint has dried, attach the background to the bulletin board, and then add the students' pasta pot pictures.

Art Concepts and Techniques

Compare the whimsical, lighter-than-air expressions on De Paola's characters to figures painted by Paul Klee and Marc Chagall.

Related Artists

Wax resist
Drawing
Painting
Watercolor wash

Beauty and the Beast

Illustrated and retold by Warwick Hutton. Atheneum Press, New York, 1985.

Story Summary

When a merchant, who has fallen on bad times and bad weather, accidentally stumbles onto an empty but welcoming palace, he cannot believe his good fortune. He eats, sleeps and awakens refreshed to find a new cloak laid out for him. But as he is leaving, he picks some roses to take to his youngest and favorite daughter, Beauty. It is then that he is confronted with the owner of the estate, a terrible beast who threatens to kill him for the theft of the flowers. The merchant, in return for his life, promises that he will send his daughter to live with the Beast. Beauty is frightened at first, but she is content in her beautiful, peaceful surrounding and gradually because of the Beast's gentle nature, she grows to love him. When she consents to marry him, the evil spell is broken, and Beast is returned to his former self–a handsome prince.

Illustrations and Comments

This well-known French tale of magic enchantment is based on a longer story written in 1757 by Madame de Beaumont. In this version Hutton's detailed illustrations contain heavy areas of shadow painted in dark gray and blue in striking contrast to the light areas. This technique has a powerful effect and achieves a sense of great space in large rooms and gardens of the Beast's domain.

Art Activity

Beast's Beautiful Blue Bird

Materials

white paper measuring at least 36" x 6" (91 x 15 cm)
pencils
watercolors
brushes
paper towels
glue and glitter
scissors
green paper for bulletin board or display area
sky blue paper
wallpaper samples
stapler

Directions

Enjoy the story and don't miss this opportunity to touch on the meaning of true beauty within. Now look back through the story, and ask the students to guess which medium the artist used (watercolor). Note the extensive gardens of the Beast's magnificent house. How did the illustrator make these pictures look so bright and sunny? (dark washes) Look at all the animals who roam free on the grounds and notice how many times peacocks are pictured. Peacocks are thought to be very proud of their beauty and magnificent tails, which are made up of long, elegant feathers. Demonstrate how the students can draw a peacock feather shape with pencil on a long strip of white paper starting with the center shaft of the feather which runs the length of the paper and ends in several concentric circles at the tip, which resembles an eye. Add individual even lines curving out from the shaft which grow larger and more erratic at the end as shown. When the students have completed their own feathers in pencil, they should paint them with large brushes and watercolor. Have them wet their feathers first; then paint areas of blues, violets and greens next to each other and watch the colors bleed together. As they near the "eye" of the feather, have them paint it with yellows, reds and oranges using the same wet-on-wet technique to allow for bleeding. However they need to exercise great care because too much bleeding of the cool colors (blues and greens) with the warm colors (reds and yellows) will turn the beautiful feather into mud! Bleeding can be controlled by gently dabbing with an absorbent paper towel to remove some of the excess water. A small crescent of black should be added around the eye to emphasize it when the other colors are nearly dry. When the feathers have thoroughly dried, squeeze white glue in a few spots on the tips of the feathers and sprinkle glitter; then cut out the feathers.

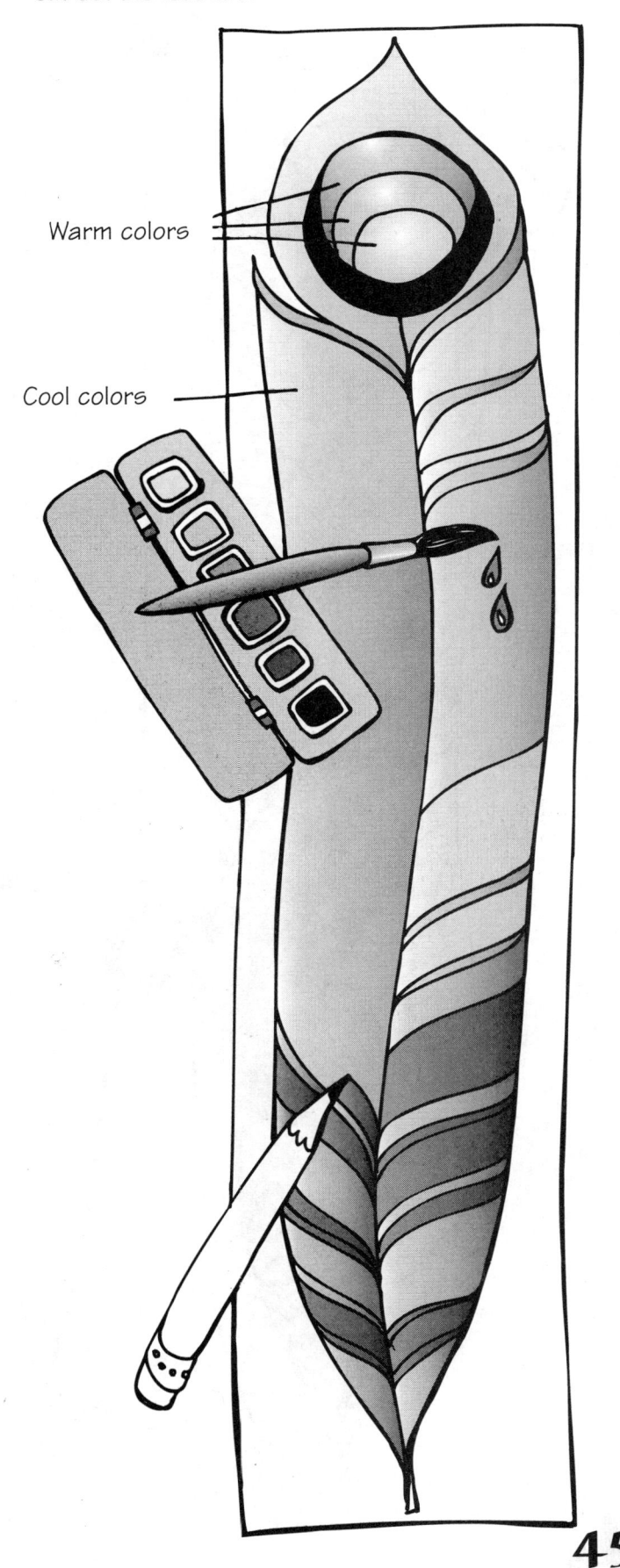

TLC10045 Copyright © Teaching & Learning Company, Carthage, IL 62321

Display

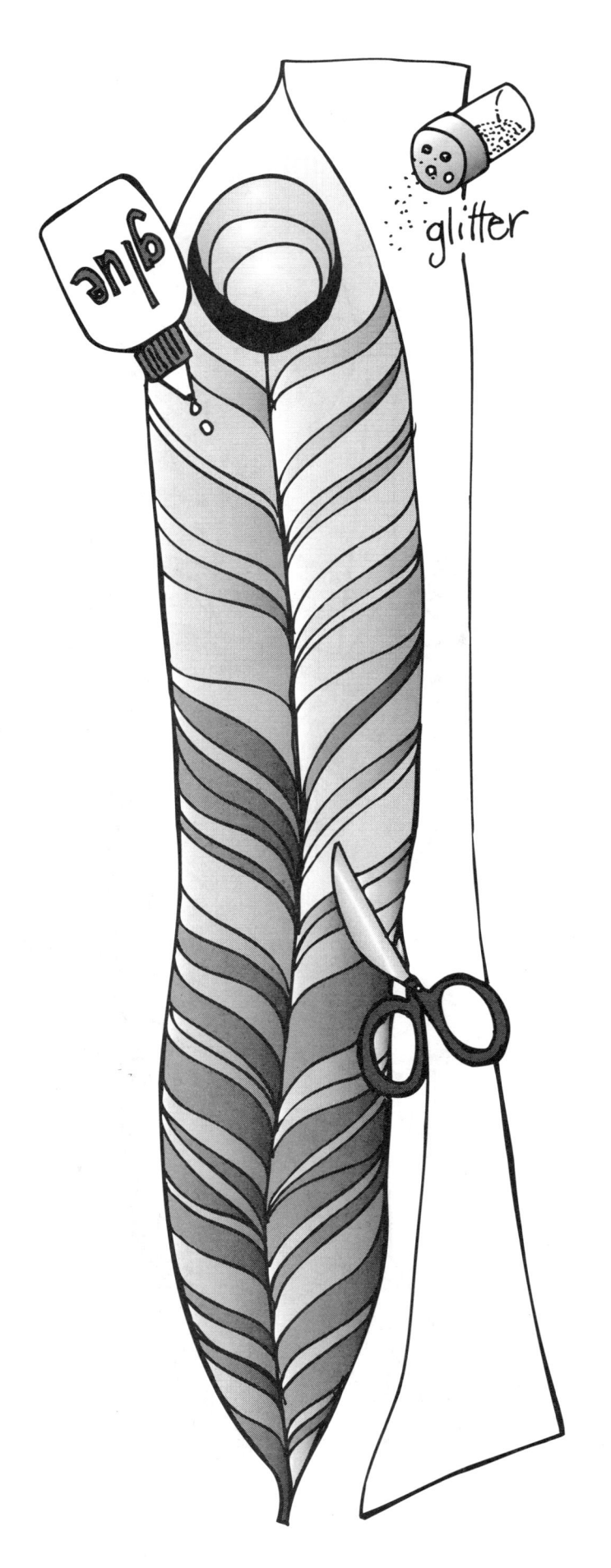

Cover the bulletin board with a sunny green background to represent Beast's vast gardens and add a 12" (30 cm) strip of blue sky across the top. Cut out fancy letters as illustrated to spell the title *Beast's Beautiful Blue Bird* out of wallpaper samples similar to the wallpaper in Hutton's illustrations. Add touches of glitter here and there to make the title and the "grounds" sparkle. Sketch a simple peacock shape in pencil on a large sheet of white paper, and use a large brush and the same watercolor wet-on-wet technique to paint the bird body blue and green allowing the colors to bleed together on the paper. Attach the letters and peacock to the background; then add the feathers created by the students. Staple these at the point where the tail meets the body, then in two or three other places, twisting each slightly so the tail feathers do not lie flat against the board but take on a three-dimensional effect. Finally, you may wish to have the students draw small figures approximately 6" (15 cm) tall of Beauty and the Beast and attach them to the display as if they are strolling through the garden in the distance. After a few days, exchange the Beast with a young, handsome prince also drawn by a student. Take a vote on which version of the Prince should remain on display!

Related Artists

The creation of beautiful gardens is an art form where the artist uses the whole outdoors as his canvas. Landscape artists develop different styles in their work just as a painter does, and the resulting gardens can move us emotionally in the same way as fine artwork can. Collect photographs of a variety of landscaped gardens (or visit one in your area), and compare these to those in the story.

Art Concepts and Techniques

Watercolor wet-on-wet technique
Drawing
Cutting
Gluing

Henny Penny

Illustrated and retold by Paul Galdone. Clarion Books, 1968.

Story Summary

An acorn plops on Henny Penny's head, and she immediately concludes that the sky is falling. She is not alone in her stupidity. For as she sets off to inform the king, she convinces Cocky Locky, Ducky Lucky, Goosey Loosey and Turkey Lurkey to join her. The addlepated fivesome never reach the king, however. They come across Foxy Loxy who shows them a shortcut to the palace–through his cave. And that's the end of them.

Illustrations and Comments

Paul Galdone's version of the English folktale was published long enough ago that the illustrations are not full-color reproductions like children's books published today so often have. Still, the art is strong and compelling, and the "birdbrains" are excellently portrayed with bugging eyes and gaping beaks.

49

Art Activity

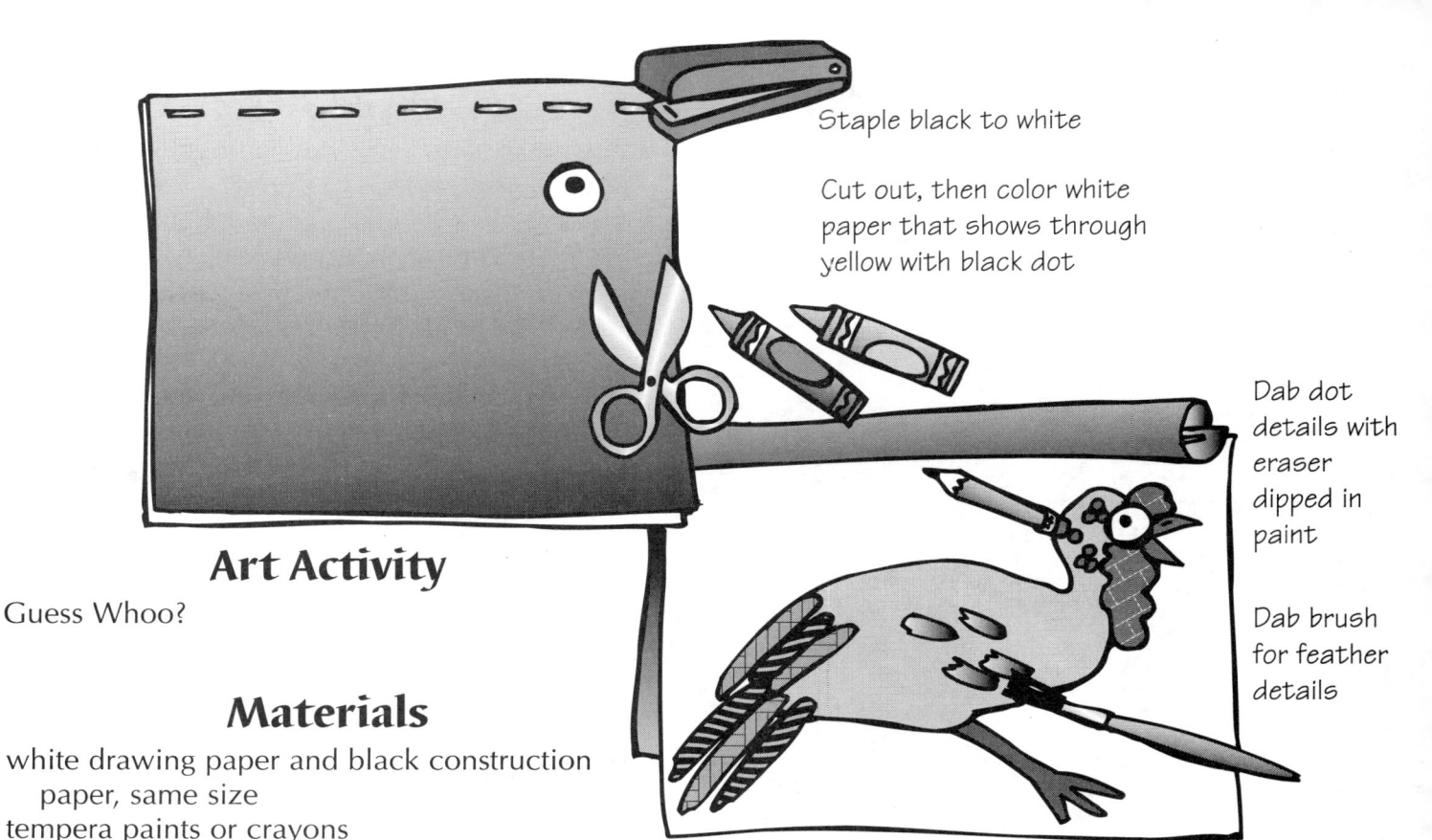

Guess Whoo?

Staple black to white

Cut out, then color white paper that shows through yellow with black dot

Dab dot details with eraser dipped in paint

Dab brush for feather details

Materials

white drawing paper and black construction paper, same size
tempera paints or crayons
pencil or sharpened stick to punch holes
stapler

Directions

Enjoy this version of the tale and discuss other versions the students may have heard. (Steven Kellogg's version has an interesting ending.) The students may have some suggestions for the fowl that could have prevented their demise. Now look back through the pages, and have the students point out similarities and differences in the five birds. Have them note the coloration of the various species; the textures and patterns of their feathers, combs and flaps; and feet. One feature which Galdone has kept the same in all the animals is the eyes. If you could only see the eyes of the fowl in the fox's cave, you would have great difficulty telling whether it was Henny Penny or one of the others. Have each student poke a hole in a sheet of black paper to represent an eye peering out from a dark cave. Staple the black sheet on top of a white sheet of paper across the top edge only, and where the white paper shows through the holes, have the students color yellow eyes with tiny black pupils. Fold the black paper back to expose the white (which now has two yellow eyes), and ask the students to paint the character of their choice around the eyes. Show them how to create the texture of the feathers by dabbing their paint-filled brush on the surface of the paper, and how to paint swirly lines for tail feathers. They can create the bumpy texture of the turkey's head by dabbing the unsharpened end of the pencil or stick in the paint and using it as a stamp. Make the students promise not to peek at the other students' artwork. Then when the paint has thoroughly dried, fold the black paper back over it so only the eyes show once more, and have the students guess which fowl is peeking out from Foxy Loxy's dark cave.

Display

On another, slightly larger sheet of black paper, paint the words *Guess Whoo?*, make the *O*s in *Whoo* the shape of two fox eyes and cut them out. Now staple a white sheet of paper underneath and repeat the activity above, only paint a fox as illustrated. Hang the fox and all the foolish fowl paintings down the hallway at kid level so that they can lift the black to see the characters beneath when they walk by.

Art Concepts and Techniques

Painting wildlife
Texture

Related Artists

Many Asian artists, ancient and modern, add washes of color over drawings done with black ink applied with brushes thick and thin. Very often the natural subject matter of these works included roosters and other birds. Paul Galdone has used a similar technique in this work to render his feathered friends. Look for examples from the Far East to compare with the illustrations in this book.

51

TLC10045 Copyright © Teaching & Learning Company, Carthage, IL 62321

Snow White

Illustrated by Angela Barrett and retold by Josephine Poole. Alfred A. Knopf, 1991.

Story Summary

The kind and good queen wished for a child with skin as white as the snow, hair as black as ebony and lips as red as the drop of blood that fell when she pricked her finger with her stitchery needle. Though her wish was granted, the queen died at Snow White's birth, and the child was raised by servants in a far wing of the castle. Her father then married a vain and cruel woman, obsessed with her own beauty. When Snow White grows more lovely than the new queen, her magic mirror relates this upsetting truth. Furious, she orders a huntsman to slay Snow White, but he takes pity on her and presents the wicked queen with a boar's heart. Snow White flees through the dark forest, terror stricken, and comes upon the home of seven dwarfs who take her in. The queen learns that Snow White is alive and living with the dwarfs through her magic mirror and devises several plans to finish her. The third attempt works as the poison apple sticks in her throat. The distraught dwarfs lay her in a glass coffin and keep constant vigil until one day a handsome prince happens by and falls in love with her. He begs the dwarfs to give him the glass coffin, and as his servants were carrying it down the mountain, one stumbles and dislodges the poisonous crumb in Snow White's throat. She wakes up immediately, marries the prince and lives happily ever after, with the seven dwarfs serving the kingdom as venerable counselors.

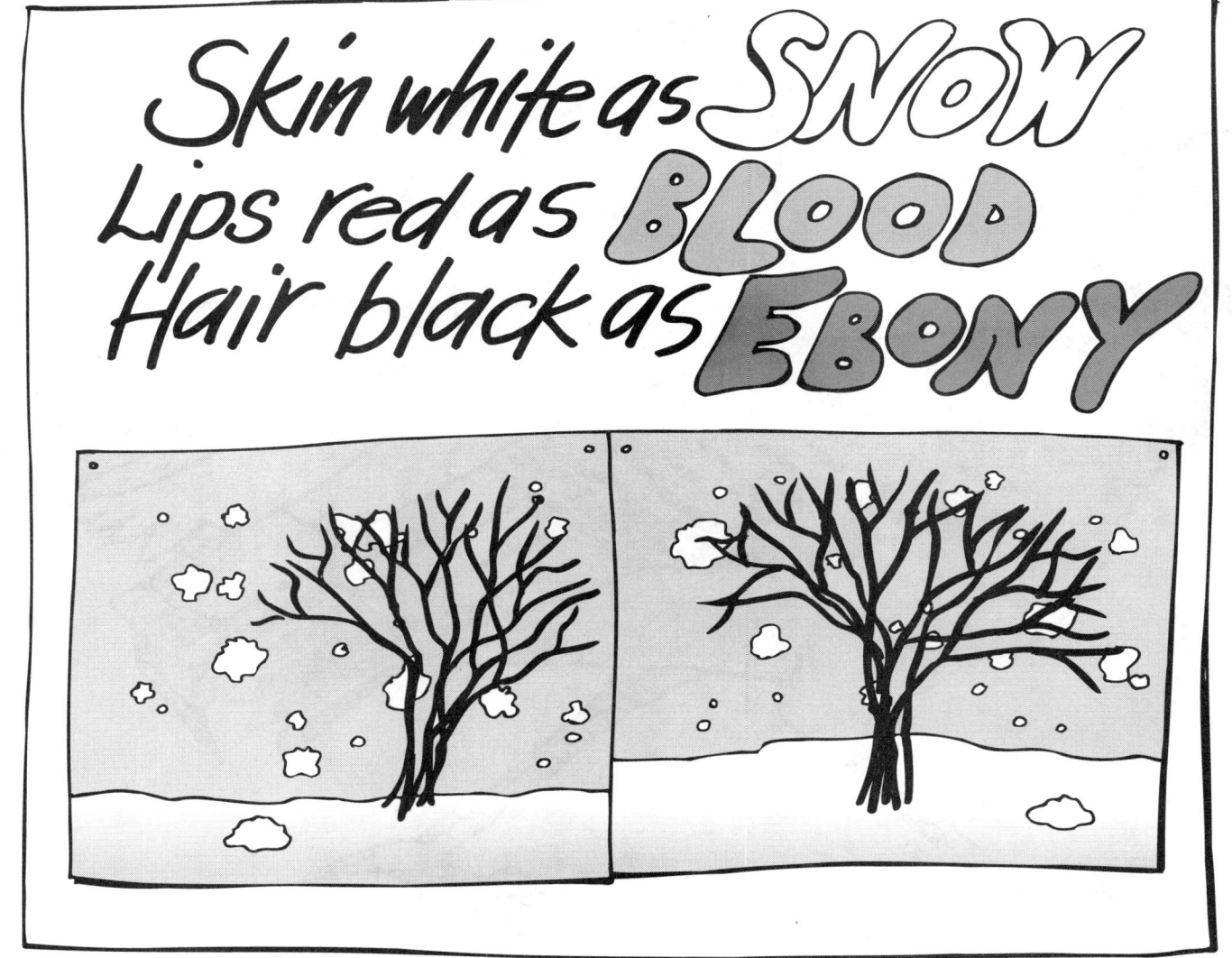

Illustrations and Comments

The illustrations Angela Barrett has done for this version of the popular German tale are as soft and deep as Snow White's own character. The queen is as loathsome as Snow White is good, and the flight through the forest is awesome. It is easy to take this story seriously with these fine illustrations.

Art Activity

Skin white as SNOW
Lips red as BLOOD
Hair black as EBONY

Materials

light blue or gray; black, white and red
    construction paper
white and red tempera
black tempera or crayon
newspapers
brushes

Directions

Read and enjoy this powerful tale with the class. Ask the class to compare this version with others they may have read. Were they more or less scary than this one? Were other versions funnier? Ask the class to recall Snow White's coloring and how it was explained in the story. Turn to the endpapers and ask the students to explain what the artist was trying to show. Now have each student create his own version of the endpaper art. On several protective layers of newspaper, lay a sheet of light blue or gray construction paper and gently "paint" it with water only until it is completely wet. Now dip the brush into thin white tempera paint and drip it onto the wet paper so that it splatters and bleeds, like a swirl of snow-white flakes. Make sure that some of the drips are large and some are small. When a pleasing amount of snow has "fallen," clean the brush and add one more drop–a bright red one. Allow these snow paintings to thoroughly dry; then using a black crayon or paint, create a leafless tree of ebony. Demonstrate how to begin at the base of the tree, dividing each branch again and again until it resembles the tree on the paper.

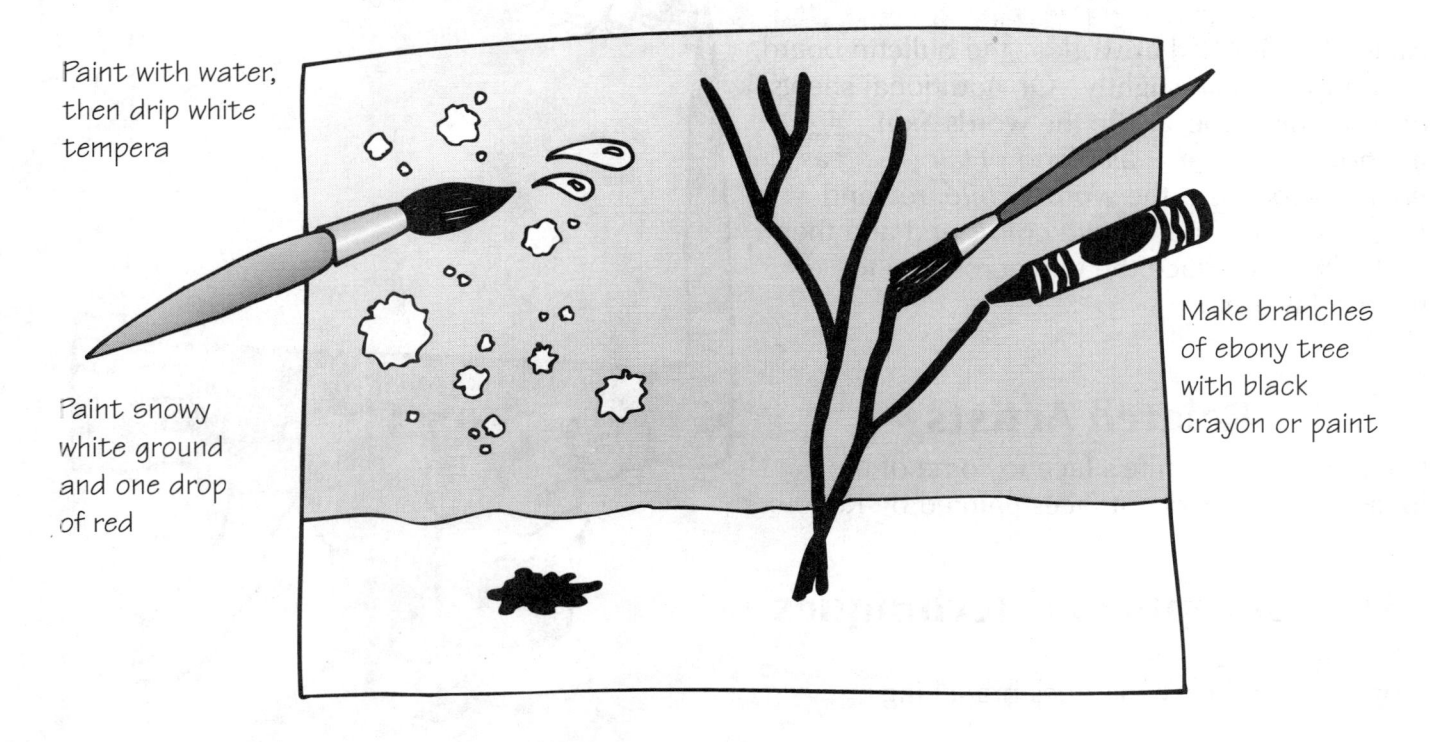

Paint with water, then drip white tempera

Paint snowy white ground and one drop of red

Make branches of ebony tree with black crayon or paint

TLC10045 Copyright © Teaching & Learning Company, Carthage, IL 62321

Display

Attach the finished artwork to the bulletin board, overlapping each slightly. On additional sheets of pale gray paper, write the words *Skin _____ as snow. Lips _____ as blood. Hair _____ as ebony wood.* Cut the words *white, red* and *black* from the appropriate colors and add them in the blanks. Place the title across the top of the display area.

Related Artists

Compare Snow White's face to some of the lovely young, innocent faces painted by Renoir.

Art Concepts and Techniques

Wet-on-wet bleeding of color
Observing and drawing trees branching

The Rainbabies

*Illustrated by Jim LaMarche and written by Laura Krauss Melmed.
Lothrop, Lee and Shepard Books, 1923.*

Story Summary

One spring night a childless couple are awakened by a moonshower, which brings good fortune to everyone it touches. They clamber outside, faces upturned to catch the raindrops and then notice a dozen tiny babies among the wildflowers. They take them in, love and care for them with no thought for their own safety and will not part with them even when offered great riches in trade. Finally, Mother Moonshower appears before them and thanks them for guarding her rainbabies. For they have truly proven themselves the worthiest of parents. They are heartbroken to lose the babies, but as a reward for their loving care, Mother Moonshower gives them a beautiful human baby girl and their happiness is complete.

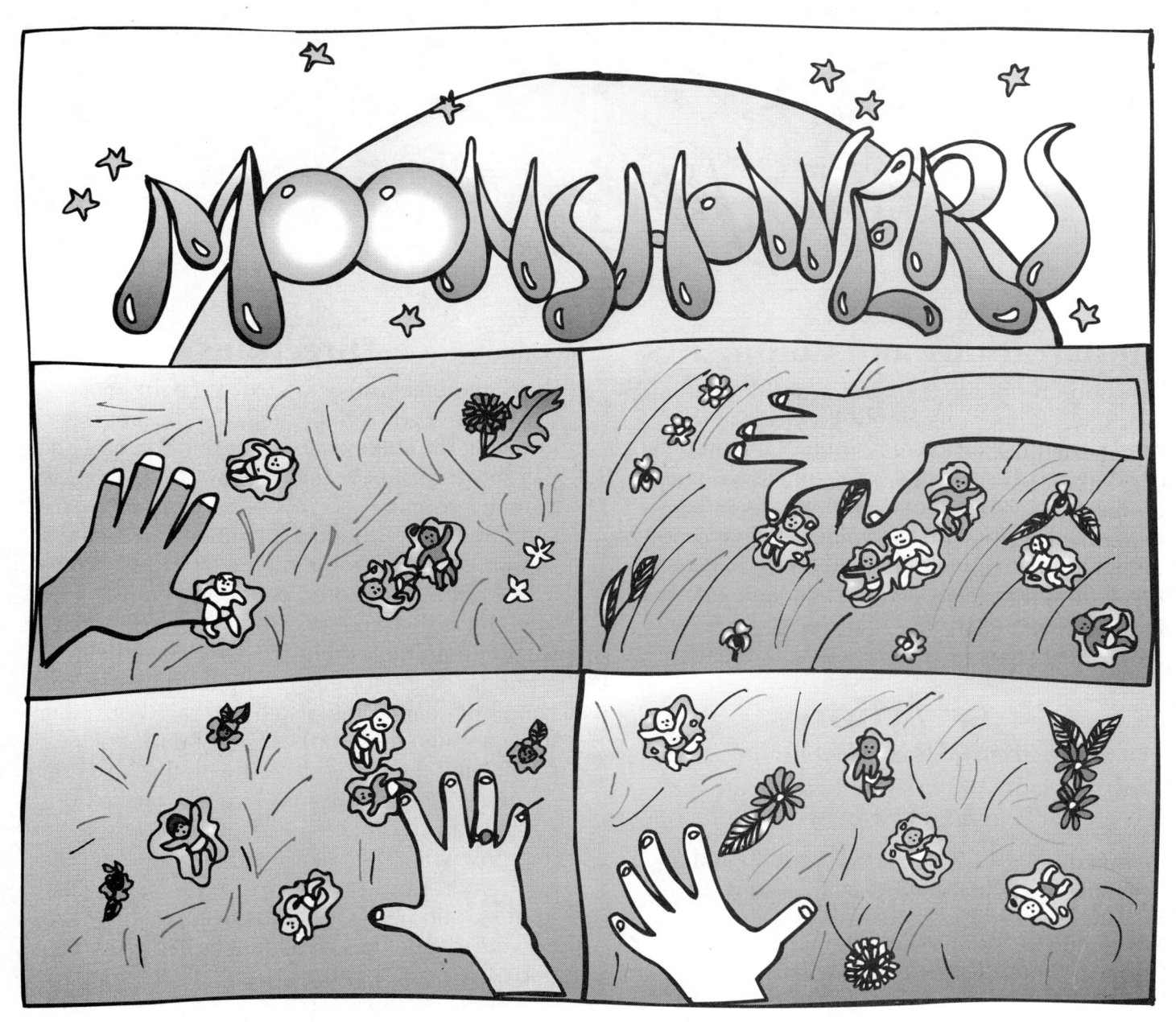

55

Illustrations and Comments

This book is not a retelling of a well-known old fairy tale. Rather it is a new story by Laura Krauss Melmed which lacks only the centuries of retelling. The illustrator sets the story in the Midwest of his own childhood, but as he says on the jacket, it could take place here and now, or "it could have happened a hundred years ago and a thousand miles away . . . Magic can happen anyplace, anytime."

Art Activity

Moonshowers

Materials

dark green, flesh-colored, yellow-gold and aqua blue construction paper
scissors
white glue
crayons

Directions

Read and enjoy this magical tale with your class. Now go back through the illustrations allowing the students to point out how the artist has shown just how tiny the rainbabies are by drawing common objects nearby for comparison. Show the students how they can create a similar comparison by tracing their own hand on a sheet of flesh-colored paper and cutting it out. Then have them cut out up to twelve tiny babies smaller than their thumbs. Next, have them cut a puddle shape for each of their rainbabies from aqua blue paper and also a few raindrops. Have them arrange these on a sheet of dark green paper until they are satisfied with the placement. Then glue them in place. Use crayons to add such details as fingernails, features on the babies and tiny white dots of reflection on the puddles and raindrops as shown. Have them add details to the ground around the babies like the leaves, flowers, dandelions and grass as shown in the book.

Display

Cut raindrop letters cut from aqua blue to spell the word *M__nshowers*. Cut two yellow-gold circles for the *O*s to represent the moons. Add a white reflection to make each raindrop look shiny, and lightly scribble some touches of orange and white crayon to add interest to the moon letters. You may even wish to add a few streaks to the sky. Place this title across the top of the bulletin board, and attach the students' artwork underneath.

Related Artists

Many of the illustrations in this book show that the illustrator, Jim LaMarche, used pastels on the rough paper as the final layer of the art. You can actually see the individual strokes, especially on Mother Moonshower. Beginning with the Impressionists, artists have left evidence of their hand in their artwork by showing brush strokes and chalk lines just as this illustrator has. See if the students can pick out the artists' strokes in the work of Degas or another Impressionist and in the illustrations of this story.

Art Concepts and Techniques

Cutting and collage
Painting "shine"
Drawing details from nature

58

Swamp Angel

Illustrated by Paul O. Zelinsky and written by Anne Isaacs.
Dutton Children's Books, 1994.

Story Summary

By the time Swamp Angel entered the contest to rid Tennessee of Thundering Tarnation, the huge and pesky bear who could "gobble up the whole winter's rations without waiting for a napkin," she was already well known for her amazing feats. All others tried and failed, but Swamp Angel preserved, wrestling that critter for three days and three nights, both awake and asleep. They snored so loud they snored down the forest. Finally, Swamp Angel snored down the last and biggest tree, which landed on the bear and killed him "dead as a stump."

Illustrations and Comments

Though this fits the recipe for a tall tale almost better than a tall tale does, it is not an old story. The author has masterfully created settings, characters and action that are so believably unbelievable, why confound it if it isn't the most wondrous heap of tomfoolery you ever did lay your eyes on. The illustrator, Zelinsky, has chosen to use an American primitive style that was common during the period when the story didn't happen. All the artwork was painted in oils on cherry, maple and birch veneers.

Art Activity

My Hero

Materials

brown paper (bags)
watercolors
pencils and Craypas™
oaktag

Directions

This story has great appeal for the kids, so take time to read it with gusto and thoroughly enjoy it. Now have the students look back through the illustrations, and ask them if they can tell what the artist used to paint on. Explain that artists do not always paint on canvas; they paint on walls, paper, glass, metal and, like this illustrator, wood veneers. Ask them to examine the wood closely for grain lines and variations of color. Different types of wood have been used, which produce a rich variation of color. Have the students try their hand at creating some wood grain of their own on light brown paper (like paper bags opened flat and trimmed). Use well-watered brown, orange and yellow watercolors with a pointed brush to create wavy lines, all running one way or folding back on each other as the wood grain in the book does. Reproduce the shape given and use it to make patterns from oaktag. When the "wood" has dried, have each student use a bright colored Craypas™ to trace the shape of his choice in the center of the wood-grained paper. Inside the shape, they should draw and color a portrait of their favorite hero, their favorite scene from the story or another tall tale they enjoy.

Display

On another sheet of brown paper that has been wood grained, trace an oval and paint *My Hero* in yellow letters in the same style as those used for the title of the book. Place this in the center of the bulletin board and the students' artwork around it.

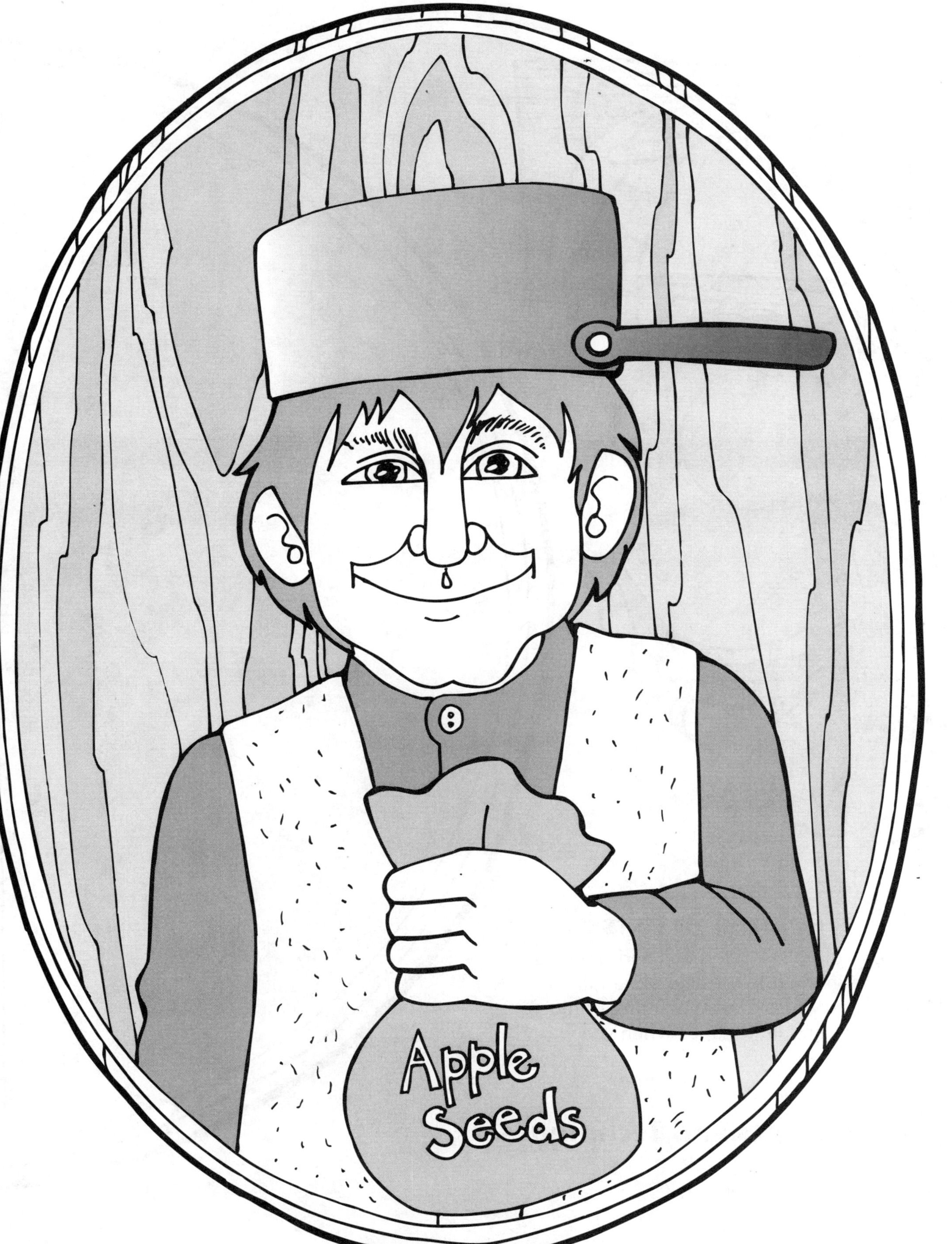
Apple
Seeds

Related Artists

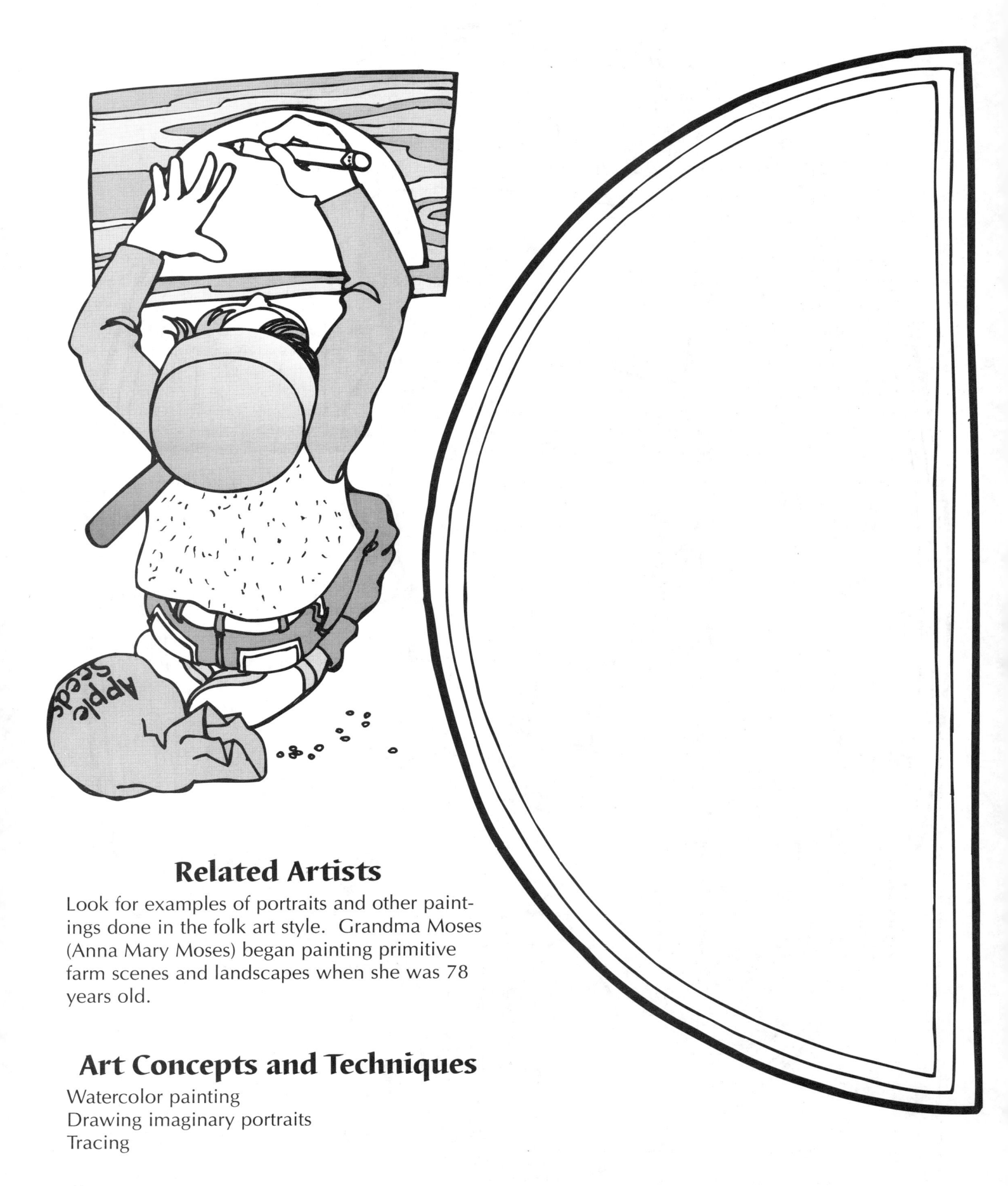

Look for examples of portraits and other paintings done in the folk art style. Grandma Moses (Anna Mary Moses) began painting primitive farm scenes and landscapes when she was 78 years old.

Art Concepts and Techniques

Watercolor painting
Drawing imaginary portraits
Tracing

Thumbelina

Illustrated by Susan Jeffers, written by Hans Christian Andersen and retold by Amy Ehrlich. Dial Press, 1979.

Story Summary

Desperate for a child, the woman planted the seeds given to her by the witch. When she gently kissed the lovely bud, it opened and there was Thumbelina, perfect in every way and only as big as a thumb. She never grew, but the woman loved her and took good care of her until one day, a frog spied her from the window ledge and thought she would make the perfect mate for her son. Here her adventures begin as she is captured by and rescued from one animal after another. When she saves a near-frozen sparrow by covering him with a blanket, he carries her far away to where she spies a field of dazzlingly beautiful flowers. She decides she could make one her home but finds it is already occupied–by a handsome fairy king, just her size, who falls in love with her on the spot, and they live happily ever after.

Illustrations and Comments

Susan Jeffers uses colored inks and dyes to draw the delicate lines of her illustrations. She begins the book with illustrations drawn at a normal distance from the action, but each subsequent illustration brings us in closer and closer as we focus on the tiny heroine. The resulting illustrations transform what we have always considered usual subject matter into very unusual forms as we adopt alternate viewpoints.

BIG BEAUTIFUL BLOOMS
(with tiny treasures)

Art Activity

Big Beautiful Blooms (with tiny treasures)

Materials

white drawing paper
colored pencils
scissors
staples or white glue
colored paper for bulletin board or display area

Directions

Enjoy this delightful story with the class, asking them to imagine what it would be like to be Thumbelina's size and sleep in a nutshell and ride on a sparrow. Think how frightening a frog would be–like meeting a dinosaur! Go back through the illustrations looking closely at the technique Susan Jeffers used. Have the students notice the fine lines which are drawn in several different directions to build up darker and darker color areas. This technique is called cross-hatching. Look at the pages with illustrations of flowers and brown leaves and how large these objects look when compared to the tiny figure. On white drawing paper, have the students use colored pencils to draw a flower or leaf as if they are as small as Thumbelina. The petals would be so large they would go right to the edge of the page and beyond. Have them color their flowers or leaves using the same cross-hatching technique as Susan Jeffers. When they have finished their big, beautiful blooms, have them draw and color one last petal on a separate sheet of paper and cut it out. On the back draw a tiny Thumbelina or her fairy king, and staple it to the artwork so that when the petal is folded back you see a surprise inside.

Staple or glue extra petal here

Display

Cover the bulletin board with any solid color except white, and use white paper to cut out fanciful letters that spell *BIG BEAUTIFUL BLOOMS*. Have students who finish early color these with all shades of pastel flower colors. Cut small letters from black or another dark shade to spell *(with tiny treasures)*. Place all the letters and the students' artwork at happy angles on the bulletin board.

Related Artists

Many artists change the size of ordinary objects to create extraordinary effects. Among them is Georgia O'Keeffe, who focused on flowers and magnified them to abstraction. Compare the students' finished work to that of this artist. Some class members will enjoy looking at her dead cow skulls painted in the same huge proportions.

Art Concepts and Techniques

Cross-hatching
Cutting
The importance of proportion in art

The Pied Piper of Hamelin

Illustrated by Annegert Fuchshuber, written by Robert Browning and retold by Barbara Bartos-Höppner. J.B. Lippincott, 1987.

Story Summary

The village of Hamelin, terribly plagued by rats in the year 1284, thought their problems were solved when a strange pied piper, dressed in a multicolored suit, offered to rid the town of their infestation for a hundred gold pieces. The Town Council agrees, and the piper led the town's rats and mice away playing a strange tune such as the townsfolk had never heard before. When the deed is done the town rejoices, singing and dancing in the marketplace, but when the time arrives to pay the piper, the mayor and corporation back down and refuse to pay the fee they promised, sending the piper on his way. He returns later, however, and plays another tune. This time all the children follow him. Though the people of Hamelin now regret their mistake, it is too late and they are never to see their beloved children again.

Illustrations and Comments

It is surprising that this well-known folktale actually began as a narrative poem by Robert Browning and was first illustrated by Kate Greenaway in 1888. This particular version was illustrated by a German artist who resides in Augsburg, Germany, which is reflected in the knowledge with which she portrays a medieval German town in every detail.

Art Activity

PAY the PIPER

Materials

orange and pink construction paper
manila paper or brown paper bag
white glue
medium gray paper
pink yarn
crayons or Craypas™
chalk
scissors
stapler
sky blue, dark blue and green paper
red, orange and fuschia paper

Directions

Enjoy the story and perhaps read them some of the original poem on which this verison is based. Explain that in 1284 when this story takes place, rats were actually a problem because they carried diseases which the people did not yet know how to cure, and that people in Germany and elsewhere lived in walled cities for their protection from enemies. Now look back through the pages focusing particularly on the illustrations which show the town of Hamelin. You can see the individual houses and buildings crowded into the confines of the sturdy walls. On other pages, details of the bright orange tiles on the roofs can be seen, as well as windows of various design, some shuttered, some paned. On some of the houses, the timbers that support the structure can be seen. Have each student cut out a house shape similar to one of those illustrated from manila paper and an interesting roof shape from bright orange paper. Ask one of the students to draw the gate house with a large arched door or make this one yourself. Use dark brown to add the details of the tiles and perhaps the heavy wooden beams. Also add windows, dormers and shutters. Encourage the students to be as creative as possible–the more details they add, the more interesting their house will look. Glue or staple tile roofs to the house. Next, work on the rats. Show the students how to make simple rats as the artist did by drawing a tear shape on a piece of gray paper, and add two small circles for ears. Use black and white crayons to draw lines of fur, and add a shiny black eye, nose and whiskers. Then add tiny pink hands, feet and ears. Cut these out, clipping in around the edges until the rat looks furry, as shown, and staple a long pink yarn tail on each rat.

Display

Cover the top half of the bulletin board with sky blue and the bottom half with grass green. In an arc across the bottom, attach darker blue construction paper on which wavy lines have been added to represent the river Weser, and another curved shape of manila above the water for the wall of the city. Place the gate house in the center of the wall. Have students add the grass and trees between the river and the wall with green crayon. Now add each student's house one behind another to complete the city. Have the class artist draw a Pied Piper, or copy the one shown. Have early finishers color him with crayon. Attach the rats everywhere lining up to follow the Pied Piper. Across the sky add a few wisps of clouds by smudging white chalk. Then add the title *PAY the PIPER* or *Unhappy Hamelin* cut from red, orange and fuschia letters, to match the main character of the story.

Related Artists

Take a closer look at the architecutre of towns. Compare the city of Hamelin to cities pictured in travel brochures of Germany from your local travel agency or books about Germany from the library. Though Germany is among the most modern countries in the world, they also take care to preserve the precious architecture of their past.

Art Concepts and Techniques

Shapes
Drawing
Architecture
Texture
Cutting

70

The Bremen Town Musicians

Illustrated by Josef Paleček, written by Brothers Grimm and translated by Anthea Bell. Picture Book Studio, 1988.

Story Summary

When the old donkey's master decided to get rid of him because his strength had failed, the donkey runs away, planning to join the Bremen Town Band. On his way, he meets an old dog, cat and a rooster who are in the same predicament as he is, and they come along. As they are settling down for the night in the forest, the rooster spies the light from a nearby window. They decide that would probably be a more comfortable spot. They peer in the window and see a band of robbers gathered around a table laden with tempting food. They are hungry! They climb onto each other's shoulders and at the given signal, crash through the glass making as much noise as they can, causing the robbers to flee in terror. The animals never made it to Bremen. They liked the cottage so well that they decided to stay and live happily ever after.

Illustrations and Comments

The illustrator of this delightful version of another Grimm's fairy tale, Josef Paleček lives in Prague. His pictures are abstractly distorted, and you can see he attacks his art fiercely, laying down layer upon layer of rich color which increases the dynamic quality of the work. He takes artistic liberties with the animals' design, especially the rooster, transforming him into a work of art in his own right.

Art Activity

Bremen Buddies

Materials

crayons
watercolors
white paper
Craypas™
oil pastels
sky-colored paper for bulletin board or display area
bright-colored construction paper

Directions

Read and enjoy the story with the class. Why do the students think they called it "The Bremen Town Musicians" when the foursome never even reached Bremen? How do they feel about the treatment of the animals just because they grew old? Now look back through the pictures and have the students guess what the artist used to make them. You can see evidence of pencil drawings and paintings overlaid with rough texture of crayons or Craypas™ and sometimes additional painting over that. Definitely, mixed (up) media! Now examine those pages which show the forest, and ask the children to compare the trees drawn by the artist to real trees. Palecek has transformed mere trees into fanciful abstractions. Show the students how they can make their own abstract trees by first sketching a fanciful shape on white paper with a crayon, as shown, and painting over it with a watercolor wash. The illustrator's trees are yellow and orange, red, pink, blue, purple, aqua and only occasionally green, so be sure to have the students note this and use the same artistic license with their trees. They may also enjoy the fact that he does not always stay within the lines. He must be too excited about his work. When the trees have dried, have the children work back into them with Craypas™ adding detail and interest. When all the trees in the class forest are perfectly splendid, cut them out. Have four students or four small groups create their versions of the four animals in the story or enlarge those given here. Color them as creatively as the trees have been colored. Forest birds and even fleeing robbers may be added.

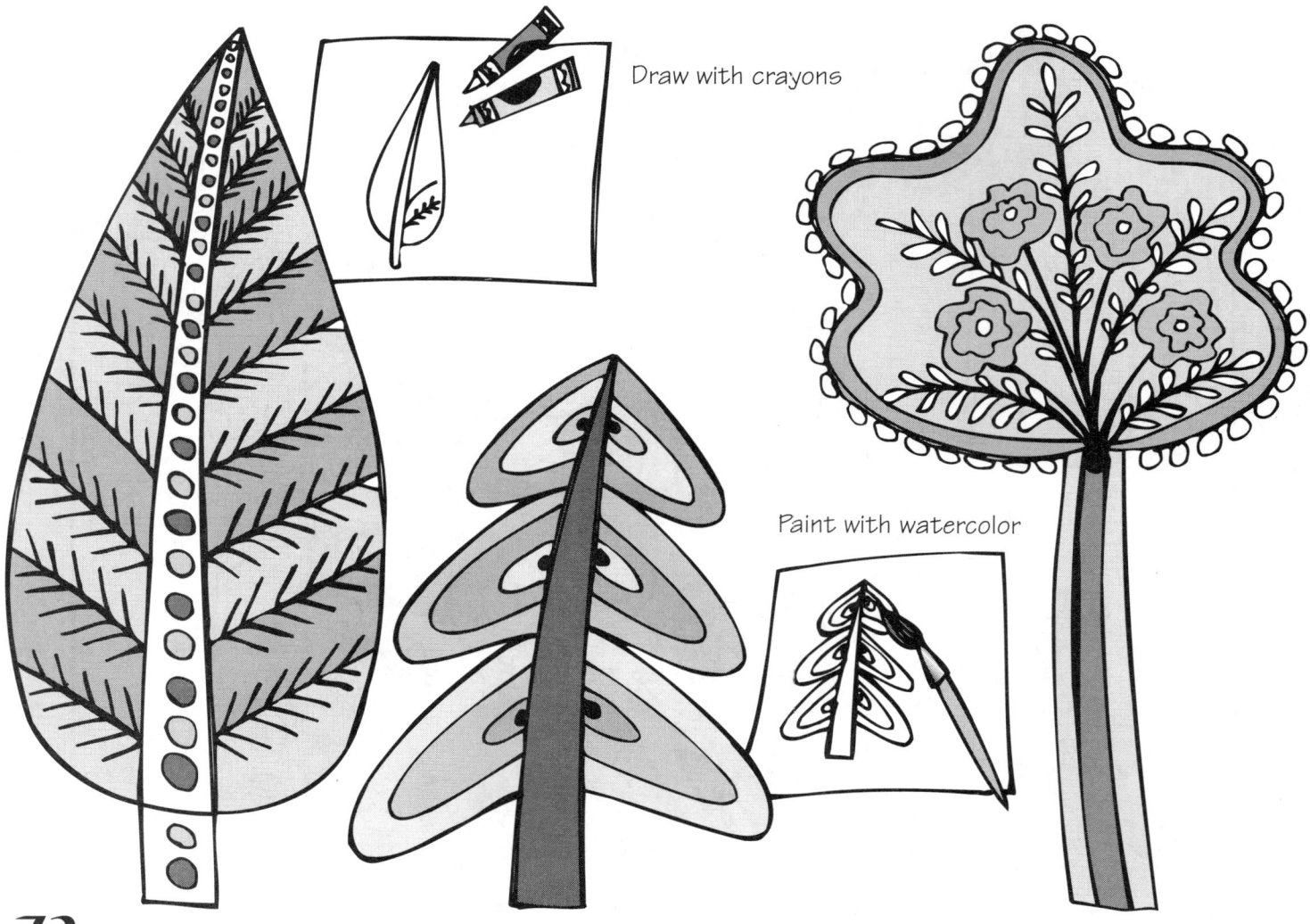

Draw with crayons

Paint with watercolor

TLC10045 Copyright © Teaching & Learning Company, Carthage, IL 62321

Display

Cover the bulletin board with an appropriate sky color. The author has again chosen every color under the sun for his skies, perhaps a pink or an orange would look nice. Attach the trees to the board to create a forest effect, leaving enough room at the bottom in front of the foliage to place the main characters of the story. Students who are not involved in drawing characters can cut out letters for the title *Bremen Buddies* from a bright color of construction paper that contrasts with the background color, and decorate these letters using the same techniques used on the trees. Place the letters across the bottom of the bulletin board under the main characters.

Related Artists

Many modern artists' works, such as Arshile Gorky's entitled *The Liver Is the Cock's Comb*, show evidence of drawing underneath that has not quite been painted over completely. The result is a dynamic piece that catches you off guard.

Art Concepts and Techniques

Mixed media
Wax resist
Painting
Drawing
Cutting

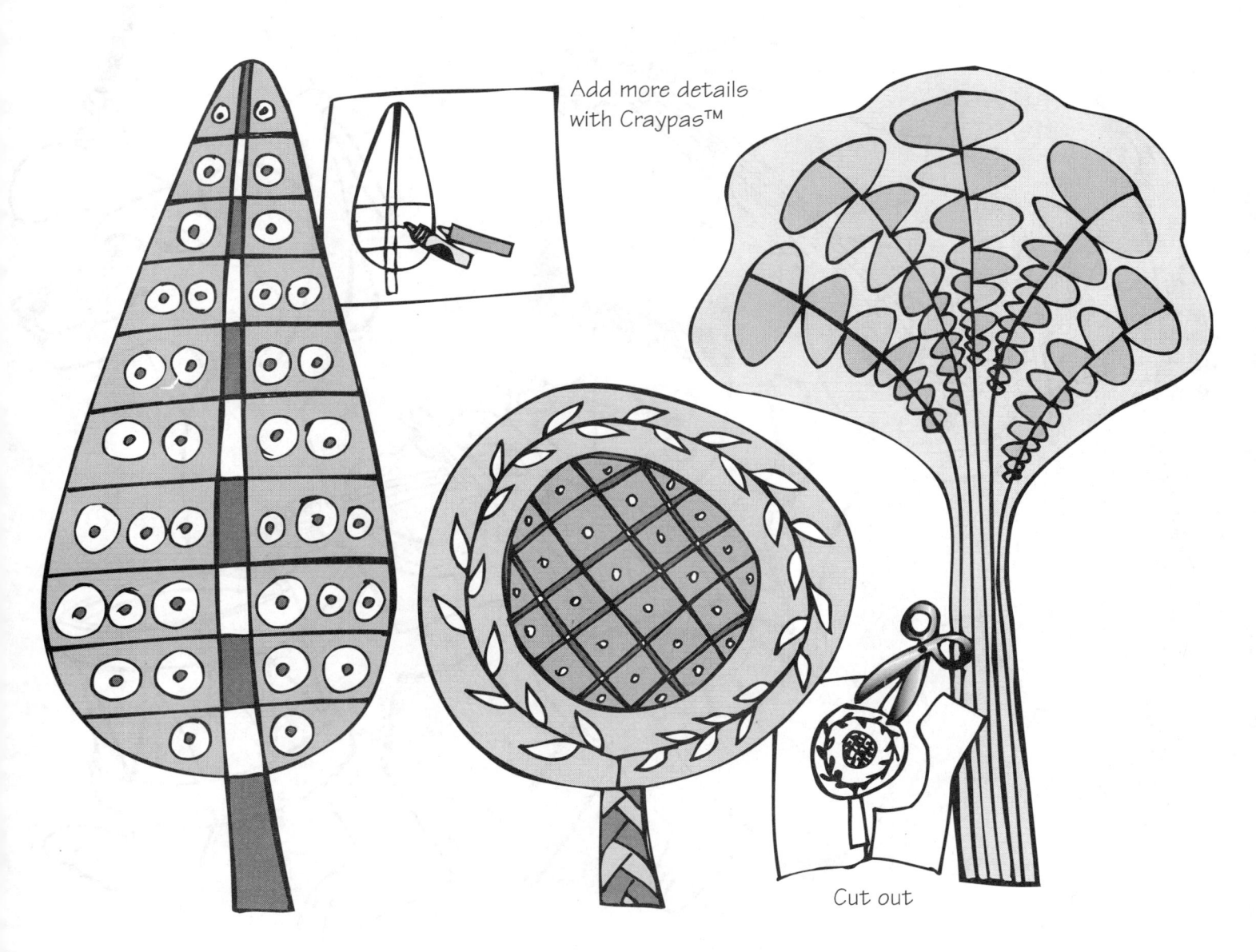

Add more details with Craypas™

Cut out

73

TLC10045 Copyright © Teaching & Learning Company, Carthage, IL 62321

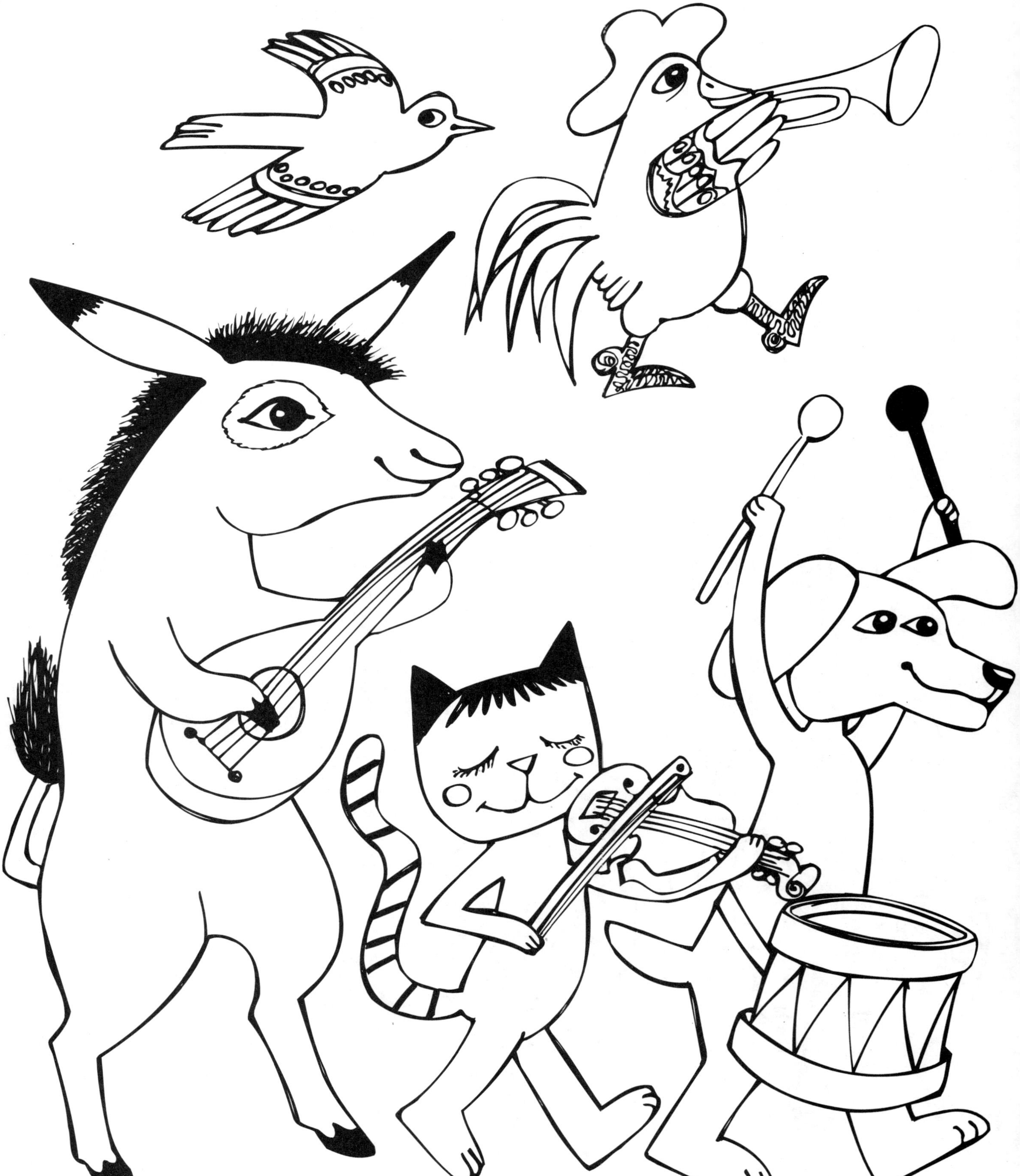

The Ugly Duckling

Illustrated and retold by Lorinda Bryan Cauley and written by Hans Christian Andersen. Harcourt Brace Jovanovich, 1979.

Story Summary

Somehow or other, a large, ugly egg has found its way into a mother duck's nest and when it finally hatches out, it looks quite unlike the other ducklings—very ugly, in fact. The poor, homely hatchling is pecked and kicked and taunted and ousted wherever he goes and must spend the long, cold winter sad and lonely among the reeds in the swamp. But during this time, unbeknown to him, a transformation takes place, and when spring arrives he finds that he is a beautiful, graceful swan. His good heart is filled with happiness because he is accepted at last.

Illustrations and Comments

The illustrator of this Hans Christian Andersen tale looks suspiciously like the girl in the duck yard who kicks the ugly duckling with her foot! She has rendered the pen and ink drawings in delicate, fine lines adding rosy washes of color, creating soft and stunning shades and color combinations.

Snowy Soft Swans Swimming

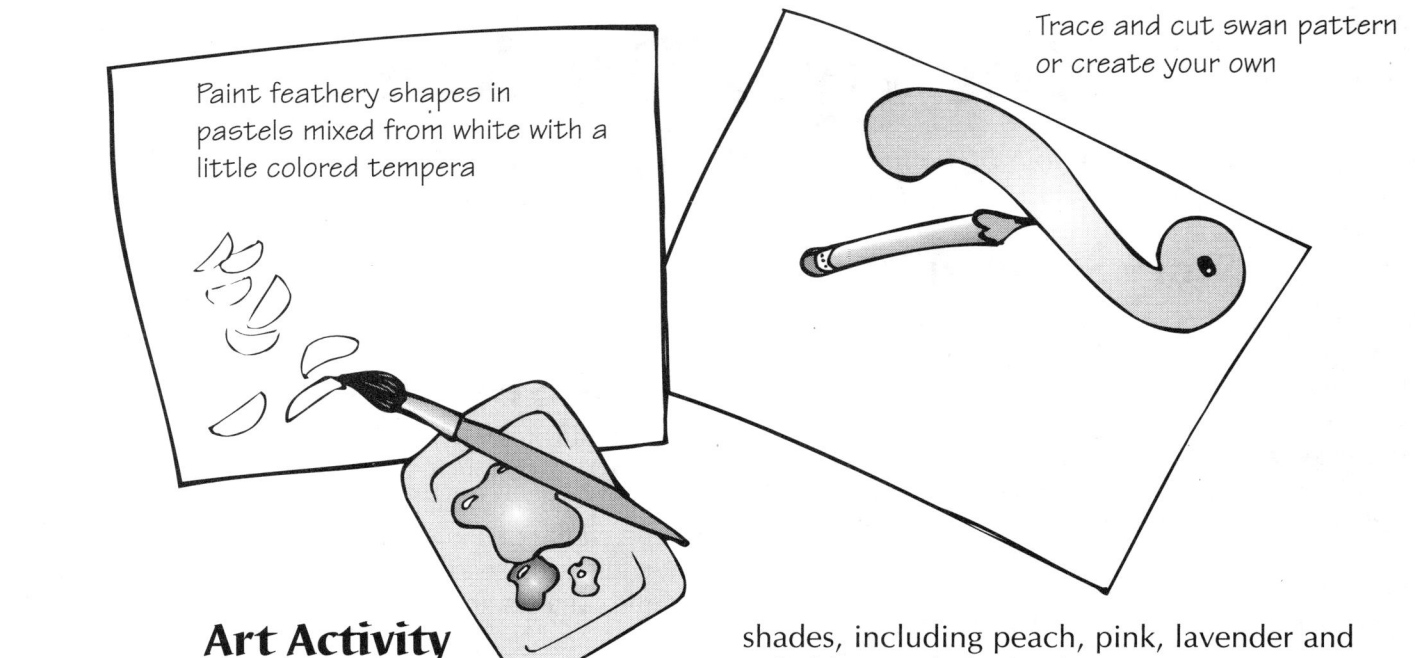

Paint feathery shapes in pastels mixed from white with a little colored tempera

Trace and cut swan pattern or create your own

Art Activity
Snowy Soft Swans Swimming

Materials
tempera paint–white and tiny amounts of other colors
brushes
Styrofoam™ trays
scissors
white glue
black, orange, white, green, purple and peachy pink construction paper
white drawing paper
magenta, turquoise and white tempera
12" x 18" (30 x 46 cm) pale blue construction paper
foil scraps
stapler

Directions
This is a bittersweet story about the pain of rejection. Read it with the students and discuss how they could prevent such an occurrence in their own class. How could they help a happy ending happen like this one in the story? Look back over the illustrations, pointing out the soft, unusual colors the illustrator has used in the fields and trees, the reeds, the other fowl and especially in the swans. While we know that swans are usually white, the artist has chosen to enhance the white with many other soft, pastel shades, including peach, pink, lavender and pale blue. Ask the students to name as many shades on a sheet of white paper using white tempera mixed with small amounts of other colors and applied in short brush strokes like the feathers of a swan's neck and back, and slightly longer strokes for wing feathers. The painted feathers will be most effective if the colors are not mixed completely but left showing streaks instead. Dip the tempera brushes into the white first; then barely touch one tip with another. The colors will blend as they are laid down on the page. Have the students fill their entire page with feathery texture. When it has dried, cut it into swan shapes as shown–long necks, bodies and wings. Assemble these shapes on a sheet of pale blue paper to form a swan, and cut out and add an orange and black beak and eye. Glue everything down and as a final touch, glue on scraps of foil horizontally on the blue so that it looks like the water sparkles. While the glue dries on the swan pictures, make some fingerprint lilacs like the ones in the final illustration of the book. Squeeze small quantities of magenta, turquoise and white tempera into a Styrofoam™ tray. Have the students dip one finger into the paint and print fingerprints onto the paper, building them up to form roughly a triangular shape like a lilac. The shape should not be perfect (check the illustration) and, as the lilacs are dry, cut them out and staple them to a leaf shape which has been cut from green and creased in the center.

Swan Pattern

Cut extra feathers from scraps

Swan's beak

Lilac leaf

Display

Staple a row of peachy pink construction paper across the top of the bulletin board and cut out white letters from your feather demonstration piece to spell the words *Snowy Soft Swans Swimming*. Cut out slightly larger replicas of these letters from deep purple or magenta and staple or glue them to the back of the white letters. Attach all the letters across the peach sky. Place the students' swans below overlapping each slightly so that they appear to be swimming in one big pond. Around the edges of the board and along the bottom, staple the lilacs, catching one end of the leaves only so that they stick out a little, creating a three-dimensional effect.

Related Artists

Find one of the paintings Claude Monet did while at Giverny–*The Water Lilies*–and examine how many different colors he used to paint the girls in white dresses rowing the boats or the lilies themselves.

Art Concepts and Techniques

Mixing pastel colors
Painting textures
Thumbprinting
Assembly of collage shapes

Cinderella

Illustrated and retold by Marcia Brown and written by Charles Perrault. Charles Scribner's Son, 1954.

Story Summary

It's the wicked stepmother again. Cinderella is so good and sweet that she makes her two ugly stepsisters look even worse then they are, so she is treated like a servant and obliged to do all the work. When the prince announces a ball, she helps her sisters prepare, never dreaming that she would be allowed to attend but wishing desperately to just the same. That evening as she weeps in her garden, her fairy godmother appears, changes the most unlikely objects into a coach, footmen, horses and a driver. Last of all she transforms Cinderella's rags into a stunning gown. She attends the ball and captures the prince's heart, but she must hurry away because at the stroke of midnight the magic spell is broken. All the magical items created by her godmother return to normal except the glass slippers, one of which she loses as she flees from the palace. The prince picks it up and vows to marry the maiden who fits the slipper. After searching the kingdom, he finds Cinderella, and they live happily ever after.

Illustrations and Comments

This story has perhaps as many versions all around the world as any tale known: "Yeh-Shen" from China, "Tattercoats" and "Mossycoat" from England, "Vasilissa the Beautiful" from Russia, "Princess Furball" from Germany, "Moss Gown" from the United States, "The Indian Cinderella," "The Egyptian Cinderella," "The Korean Cinderella". . . and so on. Though Marcia Brown's version won a Caldecott in 1954, her simple, face-color illustrations are not nearly so elaborate as the many full-color art versions which we enjoy today. Still her pictures add a silly, whimsical note to the story which seems appropriate for the life at French Court.

Art Activity

Hot Wheels

Materials

9" x 6" (23 x 15 cm) orange construction paper
12" x 18" (30 x 46 cm) medium blue construction paper
white construction paper
scissors
white glue
crayons or Craypas™
round plastic lids
glitter

Directions

Read and enjoy this version of Cinderella and have the students compare it to others they may have heard. Look back over Marcia Brown's illustrations explaining that they were done more than forty years ago. Ask the students to find examples of curlicues on each page. From the chandelier to the prince's wig, the costumes, the curtains, the architecture and the magic carriage, the illustrations are replete with fanciful curls. Now have the students focus on the carriage. If the fairy godmother can make one from a pumpkin, so can the kids! Have each student cut a pumpkin shape from a small piece of orange paper. Cut a door in it, and windows if desired, and glue to a sheet of blue construction paper as shown, taking care not to glue the door shut. Using crayons or Craypas™, trace around two round plastic lids to make the wheels, and draw spokes radiating out from a small center circle. Add swirls and curls everywhere. The more the better. Use a variety of colors and sizes. Draw a driver, footmen, and don't forget the horses. Draw ostrich plumes cascading from everyone's head. When the carriage is fit for royalty, open the door and draw Cinderella inside, enchanting in her enchanted gown, or perhaps it's the prince's carriage as he searches for the foot that fits the slipper. As a final (optional) touch, place a few dots of glue in the sky and on the carriage and sprinkle glitter.

Display

Cut out fancy letters from white paper to spell the title *Hot Wheels*, and decorate them as the carriages have been decorated, complete with glitter. Display the carriages end to end down the hall or around the room headed by the title.

Related Artists

Compare Marcia Brown's illustrations in this book with the multitude of curlicues in paintings, frescos and architectural details in palaces of the Baroque period such as The Kaisersaal; Episcopal Palace in Würzburg by Giovanni Battista Tiepolo or the Linderhoff, King Ludwig II's beautiful hunting lodge in Bavaria.

Art Concepts and Techniques

Cutting
Drawing
Tracing
The Rococo style

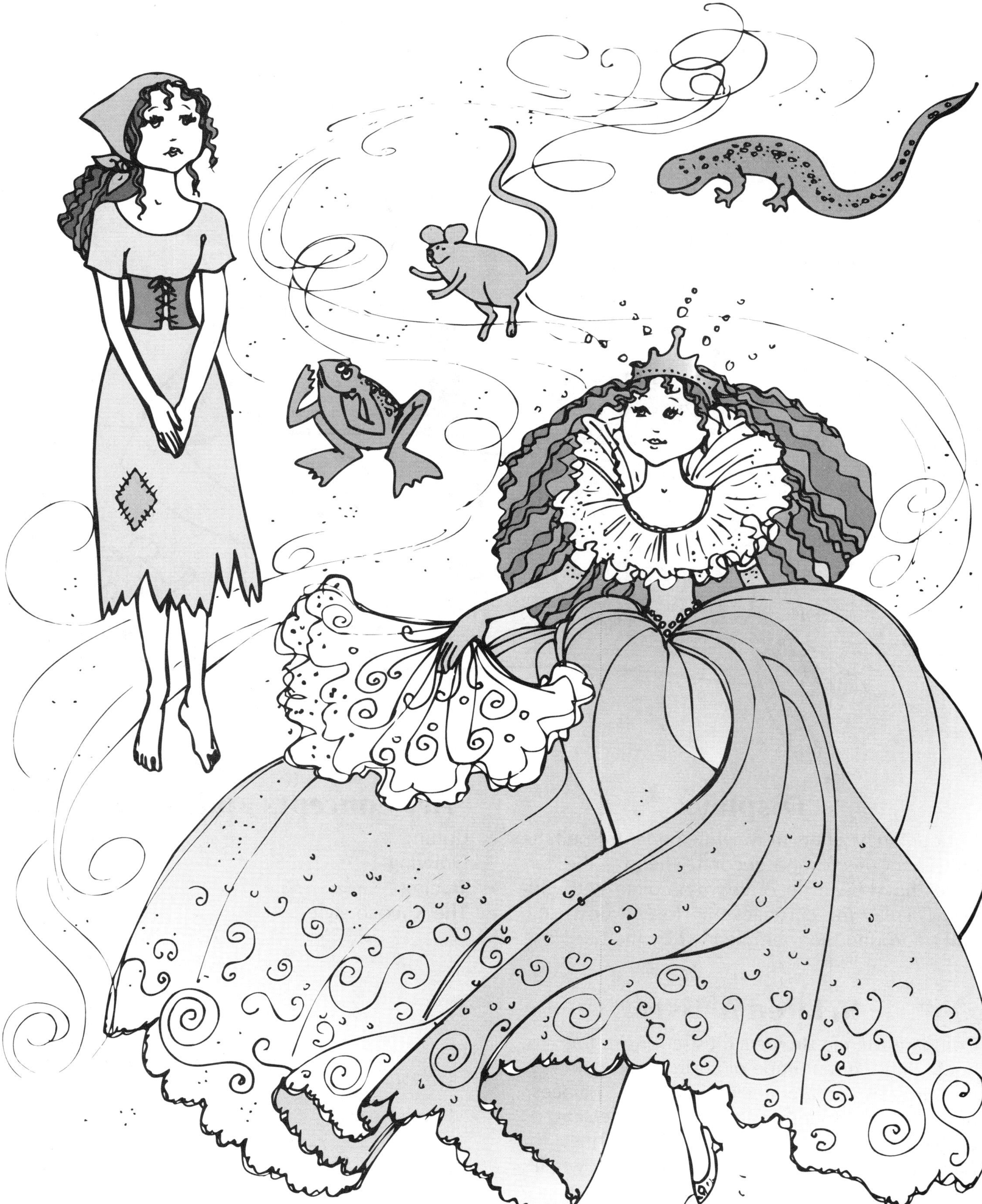

The Little Lame Prince

Illustrated and retold by Rosemary Wells, based on a story by Dinah Maris Mulock Craik. Dial Books for Young Readers, 1990.

Story Summary

They were all living happily ever after when the story began. The king and queen had just been blessed with a lovely little boy and they sat together, the queen playing her harp and the king gently rocking Prince Fransisco. But on the prince's first birthday, a foolish chambermaid dropped him and he never moved his legs again. That same night, the queen died and the king grieved so he did not live much longer. His evil brother, Osvaldo, took over the kingdom and sent Fransisco far, far away threatening his nursemaid with death if she should ever divulge his true identity to him. Time passed and Fransisco learned to read and write, but he could never walk. One day his fairy godmother appeared and gave him a magic cape with which he could fly about, and he returned home one day to learn that his nursemaid's sister, as well as everyone else in the kingdom, was suffering terribly under Osvaldo's cruel rule. Then she broke down and revealed his true identity to him. He decided, lame or not, he would save his people. Upon seeing Fransisco fly up, Osvaldo drops dead of shock (aided by the years of smoking and consuming cholesterol-laden meals), and Fransisco, though lame, rules the kingdom with his wise head and kind heart.

Illustrations and Comments

This story was first published as a novel in 1874 by an English author. In Rosemary Wells' version, all the characters are animals, and she does a wonderful job of artistically humanizing their emotions. In the illustrations as well as the story, there are no complex or subtle side plots or hidden meanings. Rather it is simple, straightforward, tender and touching, with just a touch of humor thrown in–the fairy god "pig" appears with a pop, like the sound of corn popping.

Tie ends at back

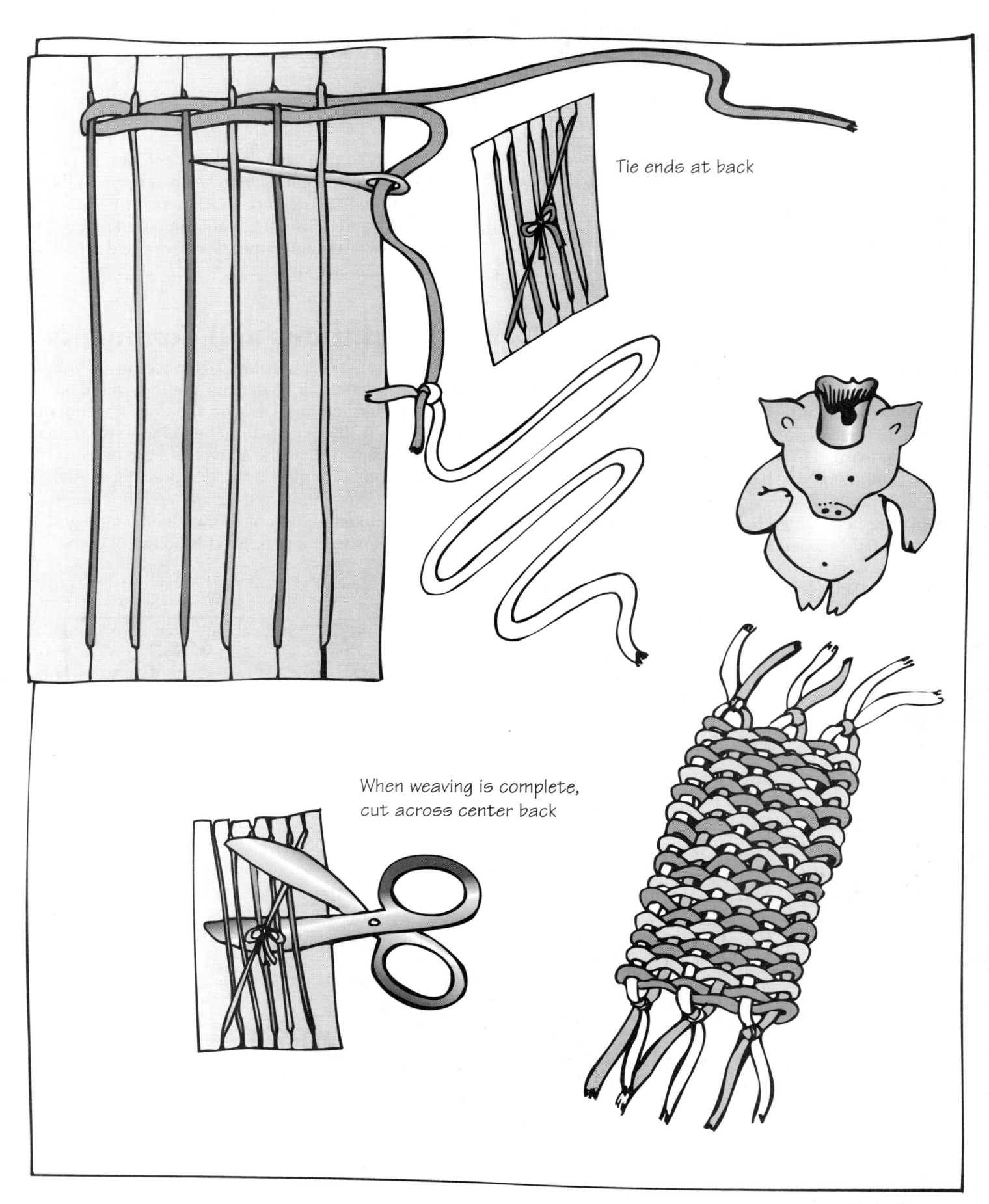

When weaving is complete, cut across center back

84
TLC10045 Copyright © Teaching & Learning Company, Carthage, IL 62321

Art Activity

When Pigs Fly

Materials

- stiff cardboard or matt board measuring 4" x 6" (10 x 15 cm)
- assorted colors of yarn—thick and thin
- plastic needlepoint needles or cardboard shuttles
- cooked or salt dough tinted pink
- assortment of colored construction paper
- foil (gold or silver)
- tape

Directions

Read and enjoy this version with the class and compare it to others they may have heard. This story presents a good opportunity to discuss physical impairments and how they need not affect our ability to do many things—including leading a country with kindness and wisdom. (Franklin D. Roosevelt was crippled with polio, but that didn't stop him.) Now turn the class' attention to the magic cape or carpet which enables the lame prince to go anywhere, and ask the class to tell of other stories where this object appears. Show the students how they can make a mini magic carpet of their own. Cut six 1/4" (.6 cm) slits in both ends of a piece of matt board and use thin, strong yarn or string to lace through the slits to make the warp threads, beginning at one side of the matt board and lacing around the back and through the second slit, and so on as shown. Tie the two ends of the string together at the back so they do not unravel. With any color yarn (weaving will progress much more quickly with thick yarn) threaded through a tapestry needle, weave over then under the six warp threads, pulling the yarn through until there is about 5" or 6" (13 or 15 cm) of it left. Turn the needle around and weave back through the warp, threading the needle under those threads which were threaded over on the last pass, and over those which were threaded under. Use a comb or pick in an upwards motion to push rows of yarn together. Continue in the same manner down the warp threads, tying new colors of yarn onto the old yarn as it is woven into the mini carpet, creating a striped effect. When the piece is woven to the bottom, cut the weaving off the matt board across the center of the back. Tie three knots across each end, each knot tying two warp threads together thus creating a small fringe. Include the extra yarn from the beginning and end of the weaving in the closest knot, then trim all the fringe so that it is even. Pull all knots through to the back of the weaving. Pinch and form a tiny pig prince from cooked clay, just the proportion for the mini magic carpet. The students may even wish to cut a tiny crown for his head from aluminum or gold foil.

Display

Of course the best way to display these would be to hang them from the ceiling as if they were flying, but then you wouldn't be able to enjoy the pig princes, so instead display them on the window ledge as if they are just ready to take off into the wild blue yonder. Cut out puffy cloud letters that spell *When Pigs Fly,* and tape them to the windowpane near the artwork. Place a small silver or golden crown atop the *P.*

Related Artists

Look at examples of rug weaving by the Navajos and other cultures. Once the students realize the work and time involved in weaving even a mini rug, they will appreciate the craftsmanship even more.

Art Concepts and Techniques

Weaving
Sculpting

Rapunzel

Illustrated by Trina Schart Hyman, retold by Barbara Rogasky and written by the Brothers Grimm. Holiday House, 1982.

Story Summary

When the poor but happy couple learned they were to be blessed with a child, they were filled with great joy, but as the expectant mother gazed out her window into the garden of the witch next door, she began to yearn for the lovely tender rampion that grew there. Soon she could think of nothing else until her husband was so worried about her health that he risked sneaking into the forbidden garden to pick some. Though he was not caught, the delicious salad the wife devoured made her want more, and her husband was not so lucky the second time. In order to escape the witch's wrath, he had to promise her his child. When the child was born, the promise was kept. The witch named the child Rapunzel and treated her kindly, but when she reached the age of 12, she was so beautiful with her long, flowing blond tresses, that the witch, loathe to share her, locked her in a high tower and barred the door. Rapunzel let her long braid out the window for the witch to climb up to reach her. A passing prince heard her singing and was mesmerized but could not get into the tower until he happened to see the witch approaching. He waited until she left, and he then used her method to enter. The pair fell deeply in love, but when the witch eventually found out, she cut Rapunzel's hair, took her far away and waited in her place, lowering the braid when the prince arrived. The shocked prince fell backward out the tower window and was blinded by the thorns beneath, wandering helplessly through the land. But about a year later, the prince once again heard the lovely singing and was reunited with Rapunzel. As she held him and wept, her tears fell on his eyes and he could see once more.

Crumple brown paper bag, open and rub with colors

Tear stone shapes and glue to tower

Cut black window and glue to the top of the tower

Cut yarn, fold in half and staple to window

Illustrations and Comments

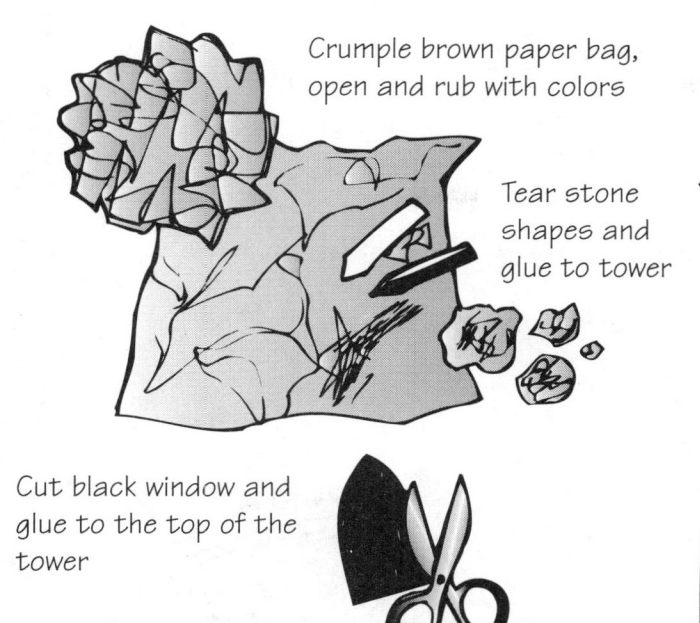

This is another of the Brothers Grimm's tales and is so very sad and melancholy a tale that it seems they deserved their surname. Trina Schart Hyman's illustrations could not fit the mood of the story any better, they are dark and mysterious. Each face fits its character perfectly and in the end, when the heroes are united, we breathe a sigh of relief.

Art Activity

Rapunzel

Materials

yellow yarn
any color 12" x 18" (30 x 46 cm) construction paper
black construction paper
brown paper bags
crayons
scissors
glue
stapler
forest green paper for bulletin board or display area
yellow or golden crepe paper or cloth
magenta construction paper

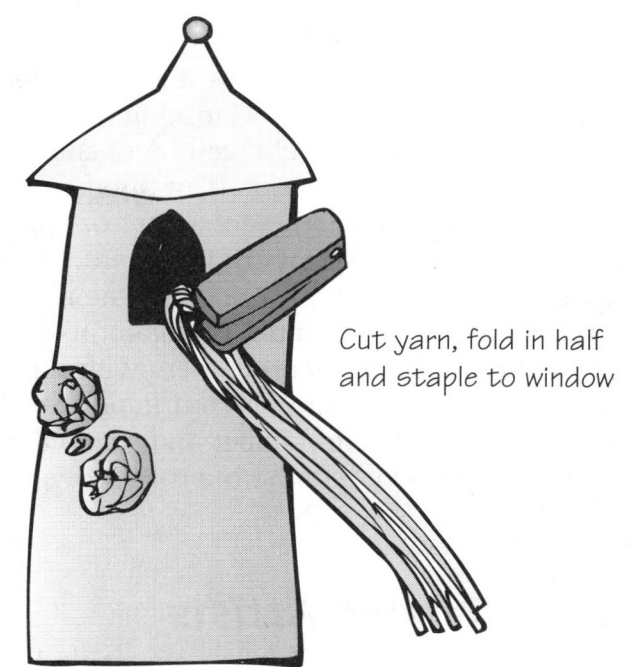

Directions

Read and enjoy the story with the class and ask the students to compare it to other versions they may have heard. Examine Trina Schart Hyman's portrayal of the witch, and ask the students if they think she looked evil in all of them. She actually was quite kind to Rapnuzel in the beginning, and the artist shows that in her portrayal. Now take another look at the foreboding tower where the witch held Rapunzel captive, especially the illustration which shows the witch climbing up her braids. Have the students draw their own towers lengthwise on 12" x 18" (30 x 46 cm) construction paper and cut them out. Be sure to have them use the full length of the paper. Next they need to make stones to cover their towers. Tear open brown paper bags so that they lay flat and crumple them up tightly then open them again. Using the sides of all colors of crayons, rub over the crumpled brown paper to accent the wrinkles and cracks to stimulate stone. Now tear small stone shapes and glue them to the towers leaving some of the background paper showing through as mortar would. Cut out one small black window and glue it way up at the top of the tower. Glue the stones around it. Use crayons to add any other details, if desired, such as the shingles on the roof. Now cut hunks of yellow yarn just over twice the distance from the window to the ground and staple it to the back of the tower window in the center of the yarn. The yarn will need to be stapled several times to be sure all the individual pieces of yarn have been secured. Divide the "hair" into three portions and braid the long tresses, tying a thin ribbon or piece of yarn (or twist tie) around the end.

Display

Cover the bulletin board with forest green paper, (The forest left over from the "Hansel and Gretel" activity would recycle well here) and attach the students' towers to it. Cut three lengths of yellow or golden crepe paper or cloth and staple it to the top corner of the board. Gently braid the three strips and drape them across the bulletin board and back again, like Christmas tree garland, securing them with staples as necessary. Cut out the word *Rapnuzel* from magenta construction paper and staple the letters to the first swoop of the braid as shown.

Related Artists

The illustrations and the story line are tangled with fiber allusions. Besides Rapunzel's woven braid and all the joy as well as grief it causes in the story, Rapunzel winds balls of yarn while the witch holds the skeins in her garden, and she weaves a rope of the silk the prince brings her, planning to use it to escape. Show and tell as may examples of weaving, knotting, braiding and other fiber arts as you and your class can think of, such as braided rugs and trims, woven scarfs and wall hangings, knitted mittens, macrame bags, etc.

Art Concepts and Techniques

Braiding
Texture for rubbings
Collage

The Frog Prince Continued

Illustrated by Steve Johnson and written by Jon Scieszka. Viking, 1991.

Story Summary

And they lived happily ever after. Well, actually they were miserable. The princess nags the prince constantly, annoyed at his frog-like traits such as hopping about all the time. The prince decides they would both be happier if he was a frog again, and sets out to find a witch who can change him back. The first witch he finds thinks he is searching for a beautiful princess to kiss and plans to cast a nasty spell on him to keep this from happening. The second witch offers him the rest of a suspiciously slimy green apple, just in case he gets any ideas about rescuing Snow White. One nibble of the third witch's gingerbread house alerts the prince, for he knows his fairy tales, but when she asks him if he's heard of two children named Hansel and Gretel, he dashes. Lost in the forest, he meets a silly fairy godmother who changes him into a carriage. Fortunately, when the clock strikes midnight, the spell is broken and as the prince runs home, he begins to think maybe he didn't have it so bad after all. Upon reaching home safely, he finds the princess has been worried about him. He kisses her and they both turn into frogs.

Illustrations and Comments

This story is so cleverly written, weaving the essence of favorite fairy tales together into a great and funny story. The illustrations are phenomenal, filled with jokes and subtleties discovered each time the book is enjoyed. The castle furnishings are all designed with a frog motif. The first witch our prince meets along the yellow brick road casts her spell using a remote control device; the second witch, "The Fairest," is reading a fashion magazine. The prince himself is a goofy looking character whose eyes bug out of his head, a vestige of his former identity. Do not keep this book for your students only; share it with fellow teachers, family members and your beloved frog, er, spouse.

Art Activity

Crazy Crests

Materials

oaktag
assortment of construction paper
white glue
crayons or Craypas™
pencils

Directions

Make sure the students are familiar with the story "The Frog Prince" before reading them this story; then read it with the class. Then go back through it slowly asking the students to identify the fairy tale alluded to on each of the pages. They may notice the yellow brick road from *The Wizard of Oz*; the witches from "Sleeping Beauty," "Snow White" and "Hansel and Gretel." After the fairy godmother turns him into a carriage, we see a big bad wolf wearing granny glasses peeking out from behind a tree. Now turn the class's attention to the frogs' family crest which is pictured above the door and on each window of the palace. Ask the class to explain why it is so well-suited to the Frog Prince, given that each partition of a crest says something of the family who proudly owns it. Have each student think back on all the fairy tales they know and choose a favorite. Without telling classmates which one has been selected, think of symbols that could be drawn on a crest that would give clues about which fairy tale has been chosen. Cut out a crest shape from oaktag using the pattern given. Glue construction paper of various colors in each of the partitions and using crayons or Craypas™, add a symbol of the tale in each partition. They might add an apple, a glass slipper, a basket, granny glasses, a house of bricks, a spool of gold . . . and so on.

Display

When the students have finished the crests, take time so the rest of the class can try to guess which fairy tale is represented, and then hang the crests in the windows of the classroom like the Frog Prince has done in his palace.

Related Artists

Find out more about art in heraldry, which first came about in the Middle Ages, when it was necessary for knights encased in massive suits of armor to be able to tell friend from foe.

Art Concepts and Techniques

Pictures which symbolize ideas

Trace outline for pattern

Crazy Crests

91

TLC10045 Copyright © Teaching & Learning Company, Carthage, IL 62321

The Dragon

*A dragon often appears in folktales all around the world.
This dragon puppet is easy to make and use in conjunction with the study of any one of them.*

Materials

five cardboard rolls
toilet paper or tissues
paper punch
newspaper
Celluclay™ or papier-mâché clay
pipe cleaners
tempera paint
sticks (chopsticks, dowels or pencils)
hot glue

Directions

Use a paper punch to make holes in each end of five cardboard rolls, stuff one with toilet paper and trim another with scissors to form a pointed tail. Use Celluclay™ or papier-mâché clay to pinch and form a dragon's head on to one end of the stuffed roll. Form bumps along the other four rolls between the punched holes taking care not to cover the holes with clay. Allow the pieces to dry, then paint them with fanciful colors of tempera adding dots, stripes and splatters for extra interest. When the paint has dried, fasten the five pieces together by lacing pipe cleaners through the punched holes and twisting. Finally, hot-glue a stick to the inside of the head and the tail piece (cut a small slit in the underside of the tail to hold the stick and liberally apply hot glue). The students can then hold one stick in each hand to manipulate the dragon through his adventures.